June 05.

IDEAS FOR
PSHE

KS1

P1 to 3

AUTHOR
Ingrid Oliver

DESIGNER
Clare Brewer

EDITOR
Clare Gallaher

ILLUSTRATIONS
Anthony Lewis

ASSISTANT EDITOR
Roanne Davis

COVER ARTWORK
Ian Murray

SERIES DESIGNER
Anna Oliwa

Text © 2000 Ingrid Oliver
© 2000 Scholastic Ltd

Designed using Adobe Pagemaker
Published by Scholastic Ltd, Villiers House, Clarendon
Avenue, Leamington Spa, Warwickshire CV32 5PR
Printed by Bell & Bain Ltd, Glasgow

67890   3456789

British Library Cataloguing-in-Publication Data
A catalogue record for this book is available from the
British Library.

ISBN 0-439-01669-X

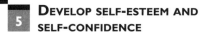

Contents

Introduction

Personal, social and health education has been recognized as fundamental in enabling children to take increasing responsibility for their own learning, and hence to maximize their potential. This style of education has been found to help children cope with social pressure affecting their learning, so raising standards of academic achievement. This in turn enhances their self-esteem and their personal health and well-being.

ABOUT THIS BOOK

Many of the types of activities in this book will be familiar to teachers. However, to facilitate curriculum planning they are arranged in a framework which is compatible with the Government guidelines for Personal, Social and Health Education (PSHE) and Citizenship for Key Stages 1 and 2 (*Preparing Young People for Adult Life*, DfEE, May 1999).

The activities will support teaching towards the four given government objectives which are to help pupils to:
■ develop self-esteem, confidence, independence and responsibility, and make the most of their abilities
■ play an active role as future citizens
■ develop a healthy lifestyle and keep themselves and others safe
■ develop effective and fulfilling relationships and learn to respect the differences between people.

Information on how to organize each activity is provided in such a way that teachers can easily adapt it to meet the needs of children of different abilities. The particular skills to be developed are linked to the National Standards for Key Skills,

with an easy-check skills index. Suggestions are given throughout for follow-up work. The activities are given within the framework of 'Outcomes of personal and social development' suggested by the Calouste Gulbenkian Foundation's PASSPORT *Framework for Personal and Social Education, Draft 4* (1998), as yet unpublished. The following eight sections have been adapted from this. They provide opportunities to enable children to:

- develop self-esteem and self-confidence
- develop a healthy lifestyle
- learn to keep themselves and others safe
- develop effective and satisfying relationships
- learn to respect the differences between people
- develop independence and responsibility
- learn to become good citizens
- make the most of their abilities.

IDEAS FOR PSHE KEY STAGE 2 (P4 TO 7)

The activities in this follow-up book are arranged under the same headings as those in *Ideas for PSHE Key Stage 1 (P1 to 3)*, and provide a built-in progression. Some activities are directly linked, so you are able to select those most appropriate for the abilities and interests of your classes.

At both stages, the activities can be integrated into a variety of curriculum areas, including healthy schools, citizenship or world of work programmes.

Section 1

DEVELOP SELF-ESTEEM AND SELF-CONFIDENCE

The activities in this section focus on children:
- expressing positive qualities about themselves and others
- recognizing feelings in different situations, what might cause them, and managing them
- knowing personal likes and dislikes
- expressing feelings in different ways and understanding their impact on others.

OUR PUPPET FRIENDS

RESOURCES AND CLASSROOM ORGANIZATION

Prepare the puppets in advance. Each child should make a happy face and a sad face sock puppet with a pair of old but clean socks; ready cut-out felt shapes of two mouths (to be attached with Velcro) and four eyes for each pair of puppets; buttons for eye centres and wool for hair; Velcro, as self-adhesive spots or strip to be cut. These can all be glued into place.

Children work as a whole (or half) class, in a circle.

WHAT TO DO

Either with the whole class, or half the class at a time, sitting in a circle, ask the children to put on the hand puppets. Explain that today they are going to talk about feelings. They each have a happy puppet and a sad puppet. *Show me your happy puppet. Show me your sad puppet.* Now ask: *What kinds of things make us happy? What kinds of things make us sad?* In each case, try to gather as many ideas as possible.

Next, ask the children to show their happy (or sad) puppet in response to a series of statements from you. *How would you feel if:*
- *it was your birthday today*
- *your friend was coming to play tomorrow*
- *your pet dog was a bit poorly*
- *your favourite television programme was on*
- *your friend was sad*
- *you can't find your favourite teddy?*

Alternatively, encourage them to show their feelings in response to a story made up by you which incorporates their ideas of what makes them happy or sad. In each case, explore the response briefly, and use words such as 'sympathy' with a sad friend, 'sharing' our feelings helps, or 'joining in' when someone else is happy (thus showing how emotions affect other people).

Finish by asking them to think about what they have just done. *What did we learn today? How did you feel about what we did?*

NOW OR LATER

- If the children seem keen to continue the activity, extend the range of feelings and vigour of the responses. For example, 'happy' could become 'very happy', 'joyful' or 'elated' (with the puppet waved about); 'sad' could become 'unhappy', 'very sad' or 'miserable' (with the puppet sagging or curling up). For the sad puppet, ask: *How can we cheer it up?* Gather suggestions. The children can then unstick the Velcro unhappy

OBJECTIVES

To enable children to:
- begin to recognize emotions and their causes
- develop a vocabulary for expressing emotions
- begin to empathize with others
- increase their self-esteem and confidence.

CROSS-CURRICULAR LINKS

ENGLISH
Responding appropriately to others; predicting outcomes; discussing; drama.

ART
Appreciating the different ways in which ideas, feelings and meanings are communicated in visual form.

mouth and replace it the other way up. Discuss ways of cheering ourselves and others up when we feel sad (showing how we can influence and help other people).

■ To reinforce the learning about feelings, children could write a list of new words to describe emotions.

■ Children could make their happy puppet talk to their sad puppet, or to other children's puppets, or to anyone else with whom they wish to develop a dialogue. When 'cheered up', the mouth on the puppet can be changed. We *can* help each other!

GIVING AND ACCEPTING PRAISE

OBJECTIVES

To enable children to:
■ express positive qualities about themselves and others
■ have the self-confidence to accept praise
■ wait patiently for their turn
■ realize the importance of valuing everyone
■ generate a positive, supportive atmosphere in the classroom.

CROSS-CURRICULAR LINKS

ENGLISH

Speaking and listening skills; responding appropriately to others.

RESOURCES AND CLASSROOM ORGANIZATION

You will need: a 'key' object which a child must hold in order to speak, for example a teddy or a ball; a sticker for each child.

Children work as a whole (or half) class, in a circle.

WHAT TO DO

Start with a class discussion about recent positive events. For example, 'Everyone behaved well and enjoyed themselves when we went swimming on Monday.' This generates a good atmosphere for giving compliments.

Move on to consider how we can give each other praise or compliments, explaining what we mean by these words if necessary. Allow the children to suggest ideas about how we can praise someone's good behaviour and characteristics (otherwise young children will tend to focus on new shoes and so on.) Ideas might be 'You are a good friend', 'You make me laugh', 'You are kind to people' and so on, so that a good quality can be found in everyone. Emphasize that the compliment must be genuine, and that they should try to be original – that is, they shouldn't just copy the previous person!

Now ask the class (or half the class) to sit in a circle. Play the following 'game': one child has the key object and praises someone else. The praised child says, 'Thank you, that was kind of you' or something similar, to accept the praise. Then the teacher gives the praised child a sticker. (This acts as a reward for accepting the praise, and identifies everyone who has had a turn at being complimented.) Everyone takes a turn to give and receive praise.

Conclude the session with a final discussion. *What does it feel like to give a compliment? What does it feel like to be praised? What might it be like to never be praised for anything? So what can we do about this? We may feel embarrassed by praise, which is natural. Even so we can respond politely, so that the person giving the compliment feels good! Praising other people helps them to feel happy about themselves, and helps us to think about the good qualities in other people.*

NOW OR LATER

■ If this activity has worked well, or if children need a regular boost to their self-esteem, this could become a weekly activity. You could reinforce the concept of giving and accepting praise by also giving praise to each child in the circle.

■ Children could make a 'Compliments chart' and ask for a sticker to put on when they have praised someone during everyday classroom activities. (You might need to limit sticker-giving to once each per day, to avoid being overwhelmed!) Ensure that everyone is giving and receiving some praise. This could be done by writing a name under each sticker.

Review the chart occasionally, and compliment the children who have been good at giving and receiving praise.

LISTEN AND REPORT

RESOURCES AND CLASSROOM ORGANIZATION

You will need: a clipboard and paper (or notebook) and pencil for each child.

Children work as a class, then in pairs. Individuals report to the whole class for discussion.

WHAT TO DO

Explain to the children that they are going to act like reporters because after interviewing another person, they will be reporting to the class about what they have found out. Each child will interview their partner about *one* subject, jotting down a few words to remind them about what has been said.

The interviews could be about:

■ my favourite topic at school
■ my favourite place to visit
■ my favourite book
■ my pet and how I look after it
■ the television programme I like best
■ my collection of…

When the children have chosen their topics, help them decide on three or four appropriate questions to ask their partner.

Allow five minutes for each interview and role-swapping, and five minutes for the reporters to consider how they are going to present their information (for example, 'This is Steven Mitchell reporting for Oakwood Primary School news…' and so on).

Each child now reports briefly to the class about their partner, saying what the topic was, and what the answers to the questions were. They then ask the interviewee how accurate the report was. If they have made a mistake, the interviewee can politely put them right!

When everyone has had their turn, discuss what the children have learned. *Were there any difficulties, and if so did you sort them out? Everyone makes mistakes – we have to accept that we made a mistake, put it right if possible, or say 'sorry', and then carry on. Did you learn anything new about your partner that you didn't know before? In talking to people we can find out things we have in common that we may not have realized before. How did it feel to be the interviewer?* (It made you feel important – you were in charge and finding things out! It was also fun.) *How did it feel to be interviewed?* (It also made you feel important – someone wants to know what you think.) *Did you find out anything about yourself that you hadn't realized before? You talked about one of your favourite things: what are your other likes and dislikes?*

NOW OR LATER

■ Children could write up their reports and present them as a class report or newspaper to show to the rest of the school or to parents.
■ Children could rehearse their interviews, or make a tape recording of them, to present at an assembly or other occasion.
■ Children could study a local newspaper report about a school or local event which they have experienced, analysing the presentation and accuracy of the report.
■ Invite the children to bring in pictures to make a poster entitled 'My favourite things'.

OBJECTIVES
To enable children to:
■ have self-insight
■ know their personal likes (and dislikes)
■ receive positive feedback
■ have support in failure
■ learn from experience.

CROSS-CURRICULAR LINKS

ENGLISH
Developing vocabulary; re-presenting information in different forms; taking turns in speaking.

WORRY WORK OUT

OBJECTIVES

To enable children to:
- develop self-insight
- recognize when they are worried about something
- begin to cope with difficult emotions and fears
- distinguish between worries about real and imaginary things.

CROSS-CURRICULAR LINKS

ENGLISH

Communicating effectively in speech; formulating, analysing and expressing ideas; discussing possibilities; drama.

RESOURCES AND CLASSROOM ORGANIZATION

You will need: a copy of photocopiable page 11 and scissors, glue and paper for each child or pair (for 'Now or later' activity).

Children work as a whole class.

WHAT TO DO

Children need to know that everyone has worries, and that this is quite normal. This activity aims to give children skills for sorting out their worries by identifying who they can approach and how, if they need help.

Explain to the children that they are going to be talking about worries. Everyone has worries, it's quite normal, but we need to know how we can sort them out. First, tell them that they are going to listen to a story:

WENDY AND WILLIAM'S WORRIES WORKED OUT

Wendy and William are twins. They have just moved house and are worried about starting their new school. They are afraid that because they are new, nobody will play with them at playtime and they might not know what to do at lunchtime.

Today they are going along to the new school for the first time. Their new teacher, Mrs Bradley, comes out into the playground to meet them. She smiles and says, 'Welcome to Waterford Primary School'. The bell goes and everyone quickly lines up in their classes. Wendy and William see lots of faces they don't know. They both have 'butterflies' in their tummies and William even feels a bit sick.

The class goes in and everyone hangs up their coats. They sit down quietly on the carpet. Then, to the twins' surprise, Mrs Bradley introduces them. 'Class Two, here are William and Wendy who are new today. I expect everyone to make them feel welcome and look after them. Now, we need some children to be their special friends, to make sure they know what to do and where to go today.' Immediately lots of hands shoot up! Mrs Bradley chooses Ryan and Preetpal because they are friendly and sensible and will take good care of the new children.

'Will they stay with us in the playground?' asks William.

'We don't know anyone and won't have anybody to play with,' says Wendy.

'Oh yes,' says Mrs Bradley, 'don't worry, they will stay with you all day, everywhere you go, won't you children?' Preetpal and Ryan nod and smile.

The day goes well, and Wendy and William find that lots of children come to talk to them and show them where things are.

At the end of the afternoon, their big brother Barry comes to pick them up from school and Mrs Bradley tells him how well the twins have got on on their first day. She also tells Barry that they had been worried about playtimes.

'Oh! I didn't realize,' says Barry. 'You didn't say anything, kids! Next time, do tell me if you are worried about something so that we can work it out together.'

'OK,' say Wendy and William, 'we will.' They both feel a lot happier now!

Discuss the story with the class: *What were Wendy and William worried about? How do we know that they were worried?* (Discuss the feeling of 'butterflies' in your tummy.) *What else might they have been worried about when they started their new school? Who helped them to work out their worries? Who could they go to if they have more worries in the future? What do you think they felt about their new school after a few weeks?*

Link the story to the children in your class. Ask them who they can talk to if they are worried about something (teacher, parent or other relative, carer and so on). Make it clear that you are available to talk to privately if someone wants to tell you something.

Then say: *Now let's talk about some of the worries that children often have and see how we can work them out together.* Talk about a worry, and ask for possible solutions. (See photocopiable page 11 for examples and possible 'work outs'.)

Now move on to discussing imaginary worries. Ask the children: *What does the word 'imaginary' mean?* Imaginary worries could be: fear of clowns or masks, characters in stories, songs or on television, fear of the dark, ghosts or monsters under the bed/in the wardrobe, or strange shapes at night. They may be able to tell you other imaginary fears/worries that Wendy or William had (to keep the discussion impersonal and confidential).

Talk to the children about ways to work out these imaginary fears, which can seem very real to them. For example, clowns and other people with make-up or masks on can be visualized taking these off to reveal the ordinary person underneath. Children can think of a 'magic' toy which could make the ghosts or monsters go away. A night light may help too! A character in a television programme could be shouted at to go away and the channel changed! The children can also think of their own ideas.

To summarize, ask the children to reflect on what they have learned about worries, and who they can ask for help if they are worried in the future.

NOW OR LATER

■ The children can cut out the boxes on the photocopiable sheet and rearrange them to match each worry with the right 'work out'. Do they know which worry is the imaginary one?

■ Children could write a list of 'People I can ask for help if I am worried'.

■ Children could write a story about someone with a worry, which ends with the worry being successfully worked out.

■ Older children could make a 'Worry question box' to be kept on the teacher's desk (and only opened by the teacher). If they have a worry they feel is difficult to talk about, they could put a message in the worry box – but they mustn't forget to put their name on it! Check the box regularly.

■ Children could role-play a worry in small groups, showing the worked-out solution.

MOOD MUSIC

RESOURCES AND CLASSROOM ORGANIZATION

Select in advance some pieces of music on CD or cassette (see the suggestions in the box on page 10). You will also need: a CD or cassette player to play the music to the class; musical instruments and art materials (for 'Now or later' activities).

Children work as a whole class.

WHAT TO DO

When the children are sitting comfortably, explain to them that they are going to listen to some different pieces of music and that they will need to think really carefully about how the music makes them feel, and if it reminds them of anything.

Play a sad/calm piece of music. Ask the children how they felt and encourage them to use lots of different words to describe their feelings – 'sad', 'unhappy', 'lonely' or 'calm', 'relaxed', 'soothed', 'peaceful', 'thoughtful', 'pensive', 'sleepy' and so on. Also, what did the music remind them of? (for example, waves on a beach, a river, dreaming). Did different children have different reactions to the piece?

OBJECTIVES

To enable children to:
■ express feelings and emotions in different ways
■ understand what triggers some feelings
■ recognize and name different feelings
■ start to manage feelings and emotions positively
■ recognize that people may respond in different ways to the same thing.

CROSS-CURRICULAR
LINKS

ENGLISH
Formulating, clarifying and expressing ideas; describing experiences; developing vocabulary; drama.

MUSIC
Responding to music; listening with concentration; recognizing how sounds are used in music to achieve particular effects; improvise musical patterns; use sounds to create musical effects, communicate musical ideas to others; respond to musical elements and changing character or mood of a piece of music by means of dance or other forms of expression.

ART
Expressing ideas and feelings.

Now play a contrasting lively/happy piece of music. Again elicit responses about their feelings – happy, excited, joyful and so on – and what the music reminds them of (for example, a circus, a party, dancing). Talk about different reactions too.

Discuss *how* the composer has written the music to make us feel the way we do. Talk about the speed, volume, instruments used and timing of the pieces, perhaps listening to them again to generate new ideas.

Then talk about how music can affect the mood we are in. If we want to feel happy, for example at a party, we play lively music. If we are feeling tired, we might want to play some soothing, calming music. Also, if someone is tired or under stress they might not want to hear any loud, vigorous music! Can the children think of any other ideas?

End by asking the children what they have learned about music and feelings. How might they use their knowledge in everyday life? (For example, being sensitive to others by not playing their music too loud.)

NOW OR LATER

■ Children could write down the names of the pieces of music and their composers together with a description of how they felt and what they were reminded of.
■ Children could improvise their own sad/calm or happy/lively pieces of music using simple instruments, and might make up a dance or drama to go with them.
■ Children could draw or paint a picture to go with the music, which could be of a place or an occasion, or an abstract piece. This could be linked with a discussion of colours – for example, 'calm' might be pale blues or greys or greens, 'lively' might be yellows, reds and oranges. Colours too can affect our moods.
■ All the above work could be linked together for a presentation, such as at an assembly or a concert.

MUSIC SUGGESTIONS
Triumphant, happy, joyful, lively, cheerful
Handel: 'Arrival of the Queen of Sheba' from *Solomon*
The Beatles: 'Yellow Submarine'
Boyzone: 'When the Going Gets Tough' (original song by Billy Ocean)
Bizet: 'March of the Toreador' from *Carmen*

Thoughtful, relaxing, gentle, sad, soft, soothing
JS Bach: 'Air on the G String'
Mozart: Piano Concerto No 21 in C – Second movement – Andante
The Corrs: 'Little Wing' from *Talk on Corners, special edition* (original song by Jimi Hendrix)

Worry work out

■ Cut out all the boxes and match up each worry with its work out.
Ask an adult to check before sticking them down!

Worry
Simon has lost
his new toy car.

Work out
Say sorry to the teacher.
You don't get told off for
an accident.

Worry
Amy has knocked over her
painting water.

Work out
Ask a dinner
lady for help. Eat
quickly and don't talk!

Worry
Sanjay can't do
up his buttons.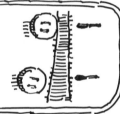

Work out
Ask for a night light. Have
a 'magic' toy which keeps
ghosts away.

Worry
Emma can't finish her
lunch in time.

Work out
Explain to Mum
and ask for her
help to find it.

Worry
Peter is afraid of
a ghost in his wardrobe.

Work out
Practise buttons at home.
At school, ask an
adult for help.

**Work out
the worries!**

The activities in this section focus on children:
- learning about factors which keep them healthy and making healthy choices
- influencing the school as a health-promoting community
- acquiring personal hygiene skills
- taking pride in their own bodies
- handling food safely
- understanding the work of health professionals.

NICE TO KNOW NOSES

OBJECTIVES

To enable children to:
- develop skills for personal hygiene
- make healthy choices
- take pride in their own bodies
- start to take responsibility for themselves.

CROSS-CURRICULAR LINKS

ENGLISH

Listening with understanding; discussing possibilities; making simple, clear explanations of choices.

SCIENCE

Learning about health and growth; understanding the meaning of being healthy.

ART

Expressing ideas.

RESOURCES AND CLASSROOM ORGANIZATION

You will need: a copy of photocopiable page 19, two postcard-sized pieces of card and two small feathers (or small pieces of tissue-paper) for each child; writing materials; a box of tissues; access to sink, soap and towels.

Children work as a whole class, then individually and in pairs, and end with a class discussion.

WHAT TO DO

Introduce the topic by discussing what we mean by a 'healthy person', and what things we can do to keep clean and healthy – washing, cleaning our teeth, taking exercise. Explain that we are going to find out more about how to keep ourselves clean, starting with… our noses! When we have a cold our noses tend to 'run'. To stay clean and help not to spread a cold, we need to learn how to blow our nose properly, by pushing the air out down our nose, the opposite of a sniff!

Give each child a tissue, two pieces of card and two feathers (or tissue-paper pieces). Ask them first to clear any contents from their noses by blowing their noses on the tissue, thinking carefully about what they are actually doing. Explain that we should always blow our noses gently so that the nose contents are not forced upwards inside our noses, rather than out. Then ask them to hold one piece of card under their bottom lip, place a feather on it and gently puff it off. Easy!

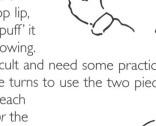

Now ask them to hold the card under their noses, above their top lip, place a feather on it and try to 'puff' it off using their noses as in real blowing. Some children may find this difficult and need some practice.

Working in pairs, children take turns to use the two pieces of card and feathers simultaneously and ask each other to puff off *either* the top *or* the bottom one.

Suggest they could demonstrate these skills at home and get other family members to try the 'feather test'. Discuss the importance of disposing of tissues appropriately and of not coughing and sneezing over other people. 'Coughs and sneezes spread diseases!'

12

Now focus on the importance of hand washing (which if done regularly and efficiently has been shown to lower the incidence of illness in school). Ask the children: *When do we need to wash our hands?* Explain that hands always need to be washed when they are dirty, and always after playing outside, after using the toilet and before eating or preparing food. Ask: *Why do we need to wash them so often?* Listen to and discuss the children's responses, but be sure that you explain that it is because we all pick up thousands of tiny 'germs' around us. *We can't see them, but if they get inside us, some of them can make us ill. Washing our hands all over with soap gets rid of germs.* Demonstrate a good hand-washing technique, including washing carefully between the fingers, rinsing and drying. Ask the children to copy this in a 'dry run', then, working in pairs, they can take turns to watch each other perfect the skill for real.

Discuss the importance of keeping *all* parts of our bodies clean – feet, hair and so on – and ask the children to fill in a copy of photocopiable page 19 using the given words (these could be blanked out for the more able children).

To reflect on the lesson, ask the children: *What have you learned about keeping clean? What are you going to remember to do to keep clean?*

NOW OR LATER

■ Each child could make a poster with a paint handprint, and if able, write underneath it 'Please wash your hands!' Older or more able children could add more detail to the message. Put these up in the toilets, by the sinks and basins, and on the dining-room doors, and so on.
■ Older or more able children could design a poster which has a 'keeping clean' message.

HEALTH HELPERS

RESOURCES AND CLASSROOM ORGANIZATION

You will need to have in advance the name of your school nurse and doctor, and to know what the local system is for their school visits (which varies in different parts of the country). You will also need: copies of any leaflets about the school health service which may be available for parents; flip chart or five large sheets of paper; equipment for measuring children's height; writing materials.

Children work as a whole class, then in groups and pairs, ending with a class discussion.

WHAT TO DO

Introduce the activity by explaining that although we can all do a lot to keep ourselves healthy, we do sometimes need extra help. *Who can give this extra help?* (Doctors, nurses, dentists.) Now ask the children to work in small groups and to discuss and write down (if they can): (1) all the places where doctors, nurses and dentists work, and (2) why people might need to go and see them.

After about five minutes, ask each group to suggest one place, and write the headings 'Doctors' surgeries', 'Hospitals', 'Clinics', 'Dental surgeries' on the sheets, as they arise, with a short list of ideas about why people might visit them there.

Now put the heading 'Schools' on one sheet. Explain that as part of the National Health Service in our country, the government provides special nurses (and doctors) to go into our schools to see every boy and girl, to give them a 'health check' to see how well they are growing.

Write the name of the school nurse on the sheet headed 'Schools'. Ask the children: *Does anyone know what the school nurse will do when she or he comes in to visit us?* (Parents and carers might be invited along too.) She or he will:
■ have a chat with each person about how they feel, and answer questions or give advice on any health worries

OBJECTIVES
To enable children to:
■ understand the work of health professionals in the NHS
■ develop confidence during health checks by school nurses
■ take a pride in their own bodies
■ start to take responsibility for themselves.

CROSS-CURRICULAR LINKS

ENGLISH
Listening with understanding; responding appropriately to others; drama – role-playing.

SCIENCE
Developing knowledge of health and growth; understanding the meaning of being healthy.

MATHS
Using purposeful contexts for measuring.

DESIGN & TECHNOLOGY
Designing skills

Ready to go! **IDEAS FOR PSHE**

- measure each person's height and weigh them
- check eyesight, one eye at a time (the other eye covered with a card) – people who wear spectacles can have them with them
- perhaps check hearing (this may be done by another special nurse or doctor).

Next, ask the children to work in pairs and think of the different ways in which we might measure someone's height (with a piece of string, when lying on the floor, standing against a wall – no shoes! – and so on). *Which method would be most accurate? How could we find out?* Different groups could then measure the same volunteers in different ways, and see how well the measurements agree.

Once you have discussed the children's results, finish the session by telling the children that the school nurse will have a very accurate method of measuring people and that they will all be interested to see what method she or he uses.

NOW OR LATER

- Invite a health professional (possibly a parent) to come and talk about their work, and answer any questions (prepared in advance of the visit).
- As nearly *everyone* will eventually use spectacles (or sunglasses), children could find out how to look after them. They could design and make a strong case, or a felt 'over case' to protect them (and make them easy to find!).

MY BODY IS WONDERFUL

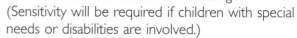

OBJECTIVES

To enable children to:
- take pride in their own bodies
- raise their self-esteem and confidence
- identify the senses of sight, sound, smell, and touch.

CROSS-CURRICULAR LINKS

ENGLISH
Learning and reciting a rhyming poem with actions.

MUSIC
Singing a song from memory.

SCIENCE
Finding out about ways in which all humans are like one another; naming senses and external body parts.

PE
Learning about the importance of physical activity and healthy lifestyles — actions can be used as a warm-up or cool-down routine.

RESOURCES AND CLASSROOM ORGANIZATION

You will need enough space for children to do the actions, including lying down; older or more able children could each have a copy of the poem on photocopiable page 20 (or copy the sheet onto an OHT to show using an OHP).

Children work as a class.

WHAT TO DO

Start by asking the children to tell you what their bodies can do, thinking about all the different parts – for example, eyes can see, blink, cry; the mouth can smile, eat, kiss, and so on. Together reach the conclusion that our bodies are amazing!

(Sensitivity will be required if children with special needs or disabilities are involved.)

Read out the poem from photocopiable page 20 (or the OHT), and give more able readers a copy to follow the text. Read it together a couple of times. Next, show the children the actions which go with it, a verse at a time (this could be spread out over several sessions), and encourage the children to learn the words. The whole class should practise reciting the poem and doing the accompanying actions. Small groups of children could demonstrate this to the class once they have learned it.

Finally, ask the children what they have learned – that their bodies are wonderful! It follows that we should take very good care of ourselves so that we can carry on being amazing.

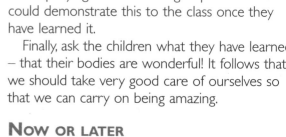

NOW OR LATER

- Children could write out the poem and illustrate it with pictures and a decorative border.

- They could learn the poem by heart and perform it in an assembly.
- Can they make up a simple tune together and sing the poem to it?
- The poem and actions could be used as a basis for a PE lesson, as a warm-up or cool-down routine. During the lesson they could do short activities which focus on the use of other body parts – hands, arms, legs, feet and so on while 'listening with their ears' and 'looking with their eyes'.
- Children might like to paint a large picture of their whole body and label all the parts, from eyelashes to toenails!

EXERCISE IS FUN!

RESOURCES AND CLASSROOM ORGANIZATION

You will need: a copy of photocopiable page 21 for each child or an enlarged version for the whole class; board or flip chart; writing materials; space for one child to mime the 'exercise'.

Children work as a class, then possibly in pairs, followed by a class discussion.

WHAT TO DO

Start by asking the children: *What do we mean by the word 'exercise'?* (Moving our body, using our muscles.) *Why do doctors tell us we need lots of exercise to keep us healthy (enough to get 'out of breath' several times a week)?* Explain that it is because they know that exercise:

- strengthens our muscles
- helps our hearts and lungs to work properly
- gives us more energy to do things.

What sorts of exercise can you think of? (Running, jogging, cycling, swimming, skipping, playing football, tennis…) Write the children's responses on the board and explain that we can use different 'action words' to describe what we are doing in each exercise. Read out the 'action words' on photocopiable page 21, and write down on the board any others that the children can suggest.

OBJECTIVES

To enable children to:
- learn about factors which help to keep them healthy and make healthy choices
- enjoy exercise
- identify many different forms of exercise.

CROSS-CURRICULAR LINKS

ENGLISH
Formulating, clarifying and expressing ideas.

SCIENCE
Learning about health and growth, the meaning of health and reasons for exercise, how exercise makes us feel; finding out about exercise out of school.

PE
Learning about the importance of physical activity and healthy lifestyles.

Answers to exercise quiz on photocopiable page 21

What exercise am I doing?	This is keeping me fit because I am…
2. football	running, kicking
3. walking/jogging/running	walking, running, swinging arms
4. cycling	pedalling, balancing, pushing
5. tennis	running, hitting
6. skipping	jumping, swinging arms

Next, *either*

read out the quiz questions from the enlarged copy of photocopiable page 21, and when each exercise is identified, write these on the sheet. Then ask one child to mime the appropriate actions. After discussion with the class, fill in the 'This is keeping me fit because I am…' section;

or

give each child a copy of photocopiable page 21 and ask them to work in pairs to complete it.

After going through the sheet, ask the children: *How do we feel after we have been exercising?* Then: *What have you learned about 'exercise'?* That exercise can be done in *many* different ways and uses different parts of the body and different skills – and can be fun!

NOW OR LATER

■ Ask the children to bring in pictures of their favourite sport or exercise and, in small groups, to share their ideas about why they like it.

■ Some groups might like to invent their own quiz and test it on others.

RELAX!

OBJECTIVES

To enable children to:
■ follow verbal instructions
■ know when they are tense
■ learn to relax and be calm and still.

CROSS-CURRICULAR LINKS

ENGLISH

Making simple, clear explanations of choices; giving reasons for opinions and actions.

PE

Learning about the importance of a healthy lifestyle – would be a good cool-down exercise after a PE lesson.

RESOURCES AND CLASSROOM ORGANIZATION

You will need to be in a hall or large room with space for children to lie down comfortably.

Children work as a whole class.

WHAT TO DO

Explain to the children that they are going to learn how to relax. Ask them: *What do we mean by 'relaxing'?* Try to get the children to realize that you let your body go quite floppy and still when you relax. *Why is this important?* Explain that if we are too tense our bodies feel 'tight' and uncomfortable. We may also get a headache.

Ask the children to lie down so that they are comfortable. Ask them to imagine they are battery driven and have just been 'switched on'. They should clench their fists and arms, screw up their faces, lift their legs off the floor slightly – any movements that tense all their muscles. Tell them to hold this for a count of three. Now ask them to imagine that their batteries have run down or have been switched off. They should let their arms and legs go floppy (their feet falling outwards), and relax their fists and face.

Now tell them to imagine that they feel really heavy, and are sinking slowly through the floor. They are breathing more slowly. Help them to think of something calm and peaceful, like lying on a quiet beach in the warm sun. Walk round the class lifting a few arms or legs to see if they are really relaxing. Tell them: *Now you should feel relaxed.*

After a minute or so, say: *Now sit up and face me again.* Ask the children: *How did it feel when you were tensed up?* (Tight, tense, clenching, gripping.) *Was this a pleasant feeling?* Help them to realize that we all need to be able to relax to stop ourselves feeling too tense. *How did it feel when you were relaxed?* (Loose, limp, heavy, calm, spread out, peaceful, happy.) *Why do we all need to relax sometimes?* Conclude that it is good for your body. It can help you to fall asleep, for example, or to calm down when you are angry.

Finally, ask: *What have you learned about tensing up and relaxing? When could you use this relaxing activity?*

NOW OR LATER

■ Compile a wordbank on the board for the children to include appropriate words when writing a piece of prose or poetry to describe their feelings about tensing and relaxing.
■ Children could draw or paint two pictures, one of themselves tensed up and one of themselves relaxed. These could be displayed on two adjacent noticeboards for dramatic effect.

TIDY UP PLEASE!

RESOURCES AND CLASSROOM ORGANIZATION
You will need: an enlarged copy of photocopiable page 22 for each child (A3 size); writing materials; dictionaries.

Children work as a class, then in pairs, ending with a class discussion.

WHAT TO DO
Explain to the children that they are going to talk about being tidy. Ask them: *What does 'tidy' mean?* (That there is 'a place for everything, and everything in its place!') *Why is it important to be tidy?* (So that we don't lose things and can find things quickly. We can look after things better and are less likely to accidentally squash or break them.) *So what might happen if we don't bother to tidy up?* (Frustration from lost items, danger of treading on sharp objects, and so on.) *What sort of places should we keep tidy?* (The classroom, the school, our bedroom, our home…)

Give each child a copy of photocopiable page 22. Discuss the picture. Is it familiar?! Ask the children to work in pairs to write down the name of an item from the untidy room in the correct place to 'tidy it up' (for example, trousers in the 'wardrobe' shape). Encourage them to use dictionaries if they are not sure of any words. Other ways to tidy up might be to make the bed, to put the lamp on the bedside table, and so on.

Discuss with the children how they have 'tidied up' the room in the picture. *Where was the lost rabbit? What have you learned about keeping tidy? What sort of containers are useful?* (Shoeboxes, cardboard boxes and so on.) *How can we use what we have learned?*

NOW OR LATER
■ Children could draw a picture of a tidy bedroom and underneath the drawing list its advantages.
■ Invite the children to write a pledge 'to keep my bedroom tidy' in the form of a signed certificate!

OBJECTIVES
To enable children to:
■ learn about factors which keep them healthy and to make healthy choices
■ learn to be 'organized' and why this is important.

CROSS-CURRICULAR LINKS

ENGLISH
Predicting outcomes and discussing possibilities; making simple, clear explanations of choices; dictionary work.

I promise to keep my bedroom tidy every day.
Signed
Samantha

HEALTHY COOKING

OBJECTIVES

To enable children to:
■ learn about factors which keep them healthy and to make healthy choices
■ learn about safe food preparation and handling
■ learn to enjoy cooking

CROSS-CURRICULAR LINKS

ENGLISH

Reading a wide range of sources of information.

SCIENCE

Learning about health and growth, different foods, the effect of heat; knowing that eating the right types of food keeps you healthy.

MATHS

Weighing.

RESOURCES AND CLASSROOM ORGANIZATION

Prepare in advance the ingredients for wholemeal scones (see photocopiable page 23). You will also need: cooking utensils, cutters, extra flour, rolling pins, bowls, spoons, a knife, weighing scales, baking trays, oven, oven gloves, aprons, wire racks, and polythene bags or boxes for the children to take scones home (plus low-fat spread or butter if the products are to be tasted!); a copy of photocopiable page 23 for each pair; adults to help with small groups of children; permission for children to taste a scone (in case of allergies, for example to gluten).

Children work in pairs, with adult help, then as a whole class.

WHAT TO DO

Introduce the activity by explaining that the children are going to do some healthy cooking. Explain that home-cooked foods may be healthier than some bought ones because we can choose not to have too much fat or sugar or salt or 'additives/ chemicals' such as preservatives, and choose to use wholemeal flour. Also, it is fun to cook, and the food tastes so good too!

Discuss why we wash our hands before cooking, and other safety issues such as hot ovens and raw eggs. (*Safety:* Ensure that the children do not taste the raw mixture or lick their fingers – raw eggs could contain salmonella.) Help the children to read out each step in the recipe before carrying it out.

Once the children have cooked their healthy scones, if possible allow them to taste them in school. Ask them: *What does yours taste like? How did you feel about this activity? Why can cooking (with help) for your family be healthy? What else have you learned?*

NOW OR LATER

■ Children could 'write up' the method for cooking the scones in their own words.
■ Suggest that the children look for other healthy recipes at home or in the library to bring into school for discussion, or possibly to cook them (perhaps for a 'Healthy evening', or an open day).
■ Children could find out more about wholefoods – what is wholemeal flour, wholewheat pasta and so on? Why are they good for us?
■ Children could grow their own healthy food such as vegetables, and even cook them. For example, carrots could be grown to make a carrot cake.

Name

Date

I can keep clean

I can blow my _____

with a hanky or _____

I love to have a shower or a _____

I _____ my

hands after going to the toilet

and before I _____

I use _____

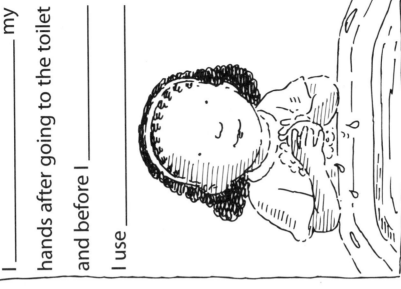

Words to choose from

bath   wash   tissue   eat   nose   soap

Name   Date

I have a wonderful body!

I can hear a whisper	(Cup hand round ear.)
And I can hear a shout	(Cup both hands round mouth.)
I can keep completely still	(Keep still!)
Or I can run about	(Run about on the spot.)

I can see my nose tip	(Touch tip of nose.)
And I can see a star	(Point up high.)
When I grow up I'll go to the moon	(Make rocket shape with arms.)
Or perhaps just drive a car!	(Hands on pretend steering wheel.)

I can stroke a pussy's fur	(Gently stroke an imaginary cat.)
And clap my hands in glee	(Clap.)
I have a wonderful body	(Arms straight up, then circle.)
And it just belongs to me!	(Both hands point to self.)

I can sit still on my bottom	(Sit.)
And I can dance around	(Dance on the spot.)
I can close my eyes to sleep	(Lie down, close eyes.)
And hardly make a sound!	(Be very quiet.)

I can curl up in a tiny ball	(Curl up very small.)
Reach my fingers up to the sky	(Reach up on tiptoe, wriggle fingers.)
I can talk and sing and laugh	(Shout ha ha.)
And wiggle my toes up high	(Legs up, wiggle toes.)

I can smell a perfumed flower	(Mime smelling a flower.)
And sniff what's cooking for tea	(Head up, sniffing.)
I have a **wonderful body**	(Arms straight up, then circle.)
And it just **belongs to me!**	(Both hands point to self.)

Name   Date

Exercise quiz

■ Choose the right exercise from box A.
■ Choose the action words you need from box B. (You may use the same word more than once.)

What exercise am I doing?	This is keeping me fit because I am...
1. I am in water, using my arms and legs. I am *swimming*	*pushing, kicking*
2. I am in a team of 11, using a big round ball. I am playing _____	
3. I can do this almost anywhere, using my legs. I am _____	
4. I am on a machine with two large wheels. I am _____	
5. I am with another person, we both have racquets. I am playing _____	
6. I am using a rope, and sometimes do this with friends. I am _____	

A	B
football running tennis cycling walking jogging skipping swimming	catching running hitting pedalling kicking walking balancing pushing swinging arms

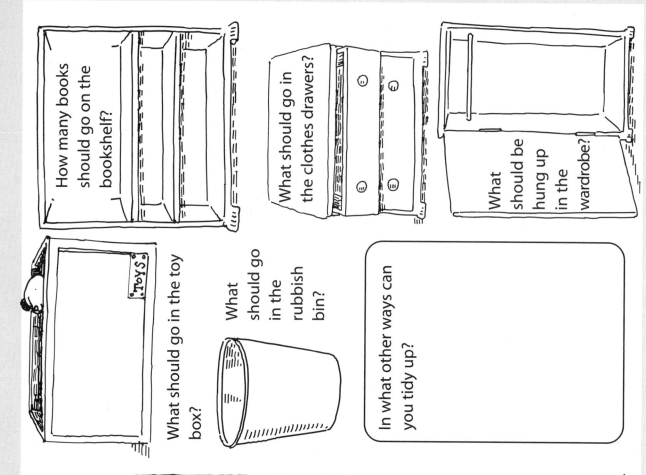

How many books should go on the bookshelf?

What should go in the clothes drawers?

What should be hung up in the wardrobe?

What should go in the toy box?

What should go in the rubbish bin?

In what other ways can you tidy up?

Tidy up please

Alex and Jo have lost a rabbit!

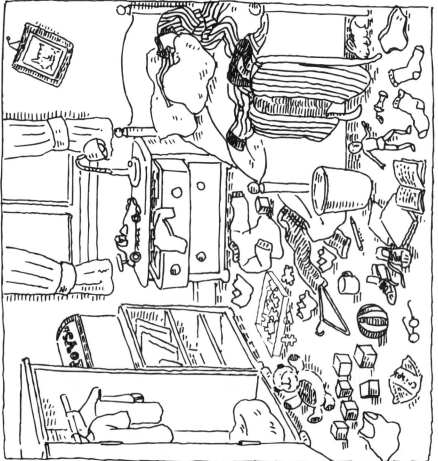

- Can you find the missing rabbit?

The missing rabbit is _____

Wholemeal scones

This recipe makes 8–10 small scones for a pair of children.

Ingredients

85g (3oz) self-raising white flour

85g (3oz) self-raising wholemeal flour

55g (2oz) margarine or butter (softened)

25g (1oz) caster sugar

55g (2oz) sultanas, chopped dates or 'ready to eat' apricots (cut into small pieces with scissors)

1 small egg

(a little skimmed milk if needed)

Low fat spread for tasting later.

Method

1. Pre-heat the oven to 200°C (400°F, Gas Mark 6).
2. Wash your hands and put on your apron.
3. Grease a baking tray.
4. Weigh out both types of flour on your scales and put them in the mixing bowl.
5. Weigh out the margarine and cut it into small pieces with a knife. Rub these into the flour using your fingertips until the mixture looks like breadcrumbs.
6. Add the sugar and dried fruit.
7. Mix in the egg and enough milk to make a soft dough, stirring gently with a knife.
8. Sprinkle some flour over your work surface and roll out the dough with a rolling pin to about 1½cm thick.
9. Cut out the scones using a small cutter (4½cm diameter).
10. Place the scones on the baking tray about 1cm apart.
11. Ask an adult to put the tray in the oven, using some oven gloves.
12. Bake them for about 10 minutes. Ask an adult to check that they are cooked (when they are firm to the touch) and if they are, remove them, with oven gloves again.
13. Taking great care as the scones will be VERY HOT, use a palette knife to move them onto a wire rack. Allow them to cool.
14. Slice one in half and spread with low fat spread. Taste it!
15. Finally don't forget to wash up with detergent and hot water (take care that it's not too hot!).

The activities in this section focus on children:
- considering hazards to health and safety
- assessing risks
- developing safety skills
- knowing where to get help
- understanding body 'rights'
- resisting pressure.

THE NAUGHTY TABLE HURT ME!

OBJECTIVES

To enable children to:
- identify potential hazards in 'inside' environments
- know what to do to keep themselves safe
- know who to ask for help
- take increasing responsibility for their own actions.

CROSS-CURRICULAR LINKS

ENGLISH

Predicting outcomes and discussing possibilities.

SCIENCE

Increasing knowledge of health and growth; using medicines safely; using electricity – awareness of dangerous sources of electricity.

RESOURCES AND CLASSROOM ORGANIZATION

You will need: a copy of photocopiable page 29 for each child; board or flip chart; paper; writing materials.

Children work in groups, then as a class, followed by individual or pair work, with a final class discussion.

WHAT TO DO

Congratulate the children on arriving safely at school and explain to them: *Today we are going to be thinking about how to keep ourselves safe in inside places.* (Home, school, shops and so on.)

Tell them that very young children do not realize they can avoid accidents by the way they behave, so if, for example, a young child runs around in a room without looking, and bumps into a table, he or she says, 'The naughty table hurt me!' As we grow up, we can learn how to avoid being hurt, and we can help other children learn as well, by being aware of what might be dangerous.

Ask the children to think of (and if possible, list), working in their groups, three inside things (tables, chairs, stairs, doorways and so on) from which they themselves need to keep safe. Ask them to discuss what the hazard is for each one, and how they could protect themselves from it.

Ask each group to tell the class about *one* of their ideas, and write the hazard and suggested solution on the board or flip chart (see opposite).

Give the children copies of photocopiable page 29. Ask them to work individually or in pairs and write their answers on a sheet of paper, using the information on the board. Check their answers.

Finally, ask the children to reflect on what they have learned. How can they use this learning to keep themselves, their families and friends safe?

NOW OR LATER

- Ask the children to design a poster of a particular hazard, to be displayed. Discuss what makes a good poster, for example bold lettering, few words, clear pictures.
- The activity could be part of ongoing work on safety, and lead on to hazards 'outside' such as water, ice, roads, strangers, building sites, railways.

Children's suggestions	Hazard	Do	Don't
Doors, stairs	Falls	Walk, look ahead, keep stairs clear.	Run, not look, leave clutter
Matches, fire, hot water, saucepans, irons	Burns	Be aware of hot things – hot water, teapot, kettle.	Touch them, sit or stand too near, pull on flexes, and so on.
Medicines, tablets, cleaning liquids, bleach	Poisoning	Check labels, only eat and drink known and safe substances. Check with adults.	Eat or drink 'found' substances, or other people's medicines or tablets.
Polythene bags, strings	Choking, suffocating	Keep small objects and bags away from babies and toddlers. Check that anoraks have no neck cords.	'Throw' food, eg nuts, sweets, into the back of the mouth, or put plastic bags over the head or put string etc round the neck.
Knives, glass, tins, sharp edges	Cuts	Treat knives, scissors and glass carefully and with respect. Get adult help on their correct use.	Leave knives, sharp or glass objects around.
Electrical plugs and flexes	Shocks	Ask for help when using electrical plugs and equipment. Turn off appliances when not in use.	Poke things into sockets, or use switches or sockets with wet hands.

HELP! I THINK I'M LOST!

RESOURCES AND CLASSROOM ORGANIZATION
You will need: a copy of photocopiable page 30 for each child; writing materials.
Children work as a class.

WHAT TO DO
Explain to the children that they are going to think about situations when they might be at risk of getting lost, so that they can learn what to do. *What does 'lost' mean? When might you get lost?* (At the shops, in the park, and so on.) *How can we stop ourselves from getting lost?* (By not running off, holding our parent's or carer's hand, listening carefully to instructions when being told to do something.)

Now read the story from photocopiable page 30 with the class, or distribute copies and let the children read it for themselves.

Ask the children: *Have you ever been in a similar situation? Do you think Simon is lost?* Amy could be just around the other side of the toy stand. *What should Simon do?* He should not panic, but stand still where he is, and call out for Amy. She will probably hear him and come over. *If Amy doesn't come, what should Simon do next?* He should find a shop assistant in uniform with a badge on, and explain who he is, and that he is looking for Amy. The assistant will announce a message over the 'tannoy' system, so Amy will find him. She must have been worried too! *What should Simon not do?* He shouldn't wander around the shop looking for Amy himself, and should definitely not leave the shop.

Following on from this discussion, encourage the children to formulate the 'rules' of how to avoid getting lost.

■ Hold hands.

■ Watch where you're going, and watch where the other person is ('keep in touch').

■ Don't go off on your own, out of sight.

If you do get lost:

■ Stand still and look around you first, then call out loudly – the person you are looking for may not be far away.

■ If you are still lost, find an adult who can help you – a shop assistant, security guard (in uniform) or a policeman.

■ If you are in a park or on a beach, ask a person (preferably a woman) for help.

■ Know your name and address and be able to say these clearly.

Finally, ask the children what they felt about the story and what they have learned about the risk of getting lost. Do they now know what to do, and how are they going to make use of this learning?

NOW OR LATER

■ Children could write their own happy ending to the story, explaining how Simon does find Amy.

■ Invite them to design a poster on the computer, giving 'Rules for not getting lost' and/or 'What to do if you are lost'.

■ In pairs, children could practise saying their names, ages and addresses slowly and clearly.

NO THANK YOU!

OBJECTIVES

To enable children to:
■ become aware of possible molestation by adults
■ develop skills to resist pressures.

CROSS-CURRICULAR LINKS

ENGLISH

Listening with understanding; predicting outcomes; discussing possibilities; drama – role-playing.

RESOURCES AND CLASSROOM ORGANIZATION

You will need: flip chart or two large sheets of paper; a hat or other item of clothing for each pair; a copy of photocopiable page 31 for each child (enlarged for younger or less able children if necessary); writing materials.

Children work as a class, then in groups and pairs, ending with a class discussion.

WHAT TO DO

Tell the children that today they are going to think about keeping themselves safe from other people. *Why do you think we need to do this?* Children need to understand that although nearly everybody is kind and helpful to children, there are a very few who could try and make children do things they don't want to. *How can we keep ourselves safe from these people?* Our bodies have got a built in 'alarm system' which can tell us if something isn't quite right. We may feel our heartbeat going up, have 'butterflies' in our tummy, or feel a bit sick or sweaty. *How else might we feel?* Write the children's ideas under the title 'Alarm signals' on one of the large sheets. *So now we can think of ways we can 'listen' to these alarm signals and get ourselves safe again.*

Ask the children to discuss in small groups what they would do if:

■ on their way home someone they knew only slightly asked them into their home, *or*

■ someone outside a shop asked them to go round the corner with them to show them where the post office is, *or*

- someone they knew asked them to do something they didn't want to do, such as kiss them or take their clothes off, and told them to keep it a secret.

What alarm signals might they feel, and what would they do to get safe again?

Discuss each group's ideas and list them on the other sheet under the title 'What to do':

- Don't go anywhere with anyone without your parent, carer or teacher knowing. Say, 'I'll have to ask my mum.'
- Say 'No' firmly, shout, run away, tell a trusted adult what happened.
- Don't keep 'secrets' you feel uncomfortable about – tell a trusted adult at once, even if you know the person who asked you to keep the secret. Do this however scared you may feel.

Explain to the children that some grown-ups they trust may be busy, or away, so they need to have several people (four or five) they can get to help them (see photocopiable page 31).

Let the children practise saying, 'No thank you', working in pairs. One of the pair tries to persuade the other to put on a hat (or other item of clothing), getting gradually more insistent, and the other resists, saying, 'No thank you' very firmly, looking the person in the eye, and meaning it! (Explain that this is 'being assertive'.) Encourage the children to use phrases other than 'No thank you' to demonstrate their assertiveness. The roles are then reversed. Praise good 'resisters' who can demonstrate their effective assertiveness to the others.

Use a copy of photocopiable page 31 to help each child to identify four or five people outside their homes whom they can trust – grandparents, friends, parents, teachers. Encourage them to role-play in pairs asking these people for help, using the sentences from the photocopiable sheet or ideas of their own.

Ask the children what they have learned about 'keeping safe'. This will summarize their findings about alarm signals, what might happen, what to do and who to tell.

Now or later

- Make sure that all the children know that they can tell you something 'in private', if they have any worries. If children reveal a situation where you suspect abuse, you must of course use the Child Protection Procedure of the school, and refer to the designated teacher.
- Display a poster with the 'Childline' number on it and discuss its use with the children.

EMERGENCY?

RESOURCES AND CLASSROOM ORGANIZATION

You will need: toy telephones, one for each child (models of conventional or mobile telephones could be made in advance by the children using appropriate resources such as boxes, string and so on); a copy of photocopiable page 32 for each child.

Children work as a class, then in fours and pairs, with a final class discussion.

WHAT TO DO

Continuing the theme of how we keep ourselves and others safe, explain that sometimes things

OBJECTIVES

To enable children to:
- learn about hazards to health and safety
- understand what is an 'emergency'
- know what to do to get help in an emergency
- practise telephone skills.

CROSS-CURRICULAR LINKS

ENGLISH

Writing in response to a variety of stimuli, including classroom activities.

happen very quickly, and we need to know how to get help urgently. Ask the children to give examples of such a situation – for example, when someone has been badly injured, or is taken ill, is in a car crash, or has fallen into a river or the sea. These are called 'emergencies'. Usually there are grown-ups around to get the needed help, but it is useful to know what to do if we are on our own. *What should we do then?* (Use any phone to dial 999.)

Explain that when you dial 999 the person answering the phone will ask whether you need the police, ambulance or the fire brigade. You should tell them, and then also give your address and *what* the emergency is. THEN STAY ON THE PHONE, DO NOT PUT IT DOWN until the person on the phone tells you it is OK to go. (Sometimes people panic and forget to say where they are!) You should NEVER dial 999 unless it is a real emergency. *Why not?* Because you might be putting someone else's life at risk, who *really* needs the ambulance or fire engine. Also, calling out the emergency services costs a lot of money.

So we have to ask ourselves: 'Is there any grown-up nearby who can help?' If not, 'Is this really an emergency and is someone's life in danger?' Ask the class to give examples of non-emergency situations, such as losing a dog, and explain that there are other services (coastguard or breakdown/recovery) we can call on for help.

Give each child a copy of photocopiable page 32 to complete working in groups of four. Read out, or ask the children to read, the 'situations', then give each group time to discuss them, deciding which are real emergencies and warrant a 999 call, and which service would be required.

Now ask the children to work in pairs and practise calling the service, choosing *one* of the agreed 'real emergency' situations described on the photocopiable sheet. A suggested dialogue is shown below.

Finally, ask them how they felt about the lesson and what they have learned about what to do in a real emergency. Reassure them that such emergencies are very rare and that there is usually a grown-up nearby to help.

NOW OR LATER

■ Small groups of children could be taken to a pay phone near the school to practise using a public phone, to call home or the school, by arrangement.

■ Encourage older children to take First Aid courses and learn about recovery positions and resuscitation techniques.

■ Members of the police, ambulance or fire brigade could be asked to talk about their work and answer questions about 999 calls.

Answers to 'Is this a real emergency?' on photocopiable page 32

1. Yes, ambulance
2. No (wait for adult help later)
3. Yes, fire brigade
4. Yes, ambulance
5. No (cover wound temporarily with a *clean* hanky or sticking plaster – wait for adult to clean it as soon as possible)
6. Yes, police

Practising what to say when you dial 999

Child 1 (calling)

1. Dial 999

3. 'Fire brigade please.' (or ambulance or police)

5. 'My name is…'

7. 'I am…'

9. 'The problem is…'

Child 2 (answering)

2. 'Hello, do you require police, ambulance or fire brigade?'

4. 'What is your name?'

6. 'Where are you?'

8. 'What has happened?'

10. 'Thank you for calling. Don't worry, the fire brigade is on its way.'

Be aware and take care!

■ Write down what it is in the picture, why it could be dangerous, and how to keep safe from it.

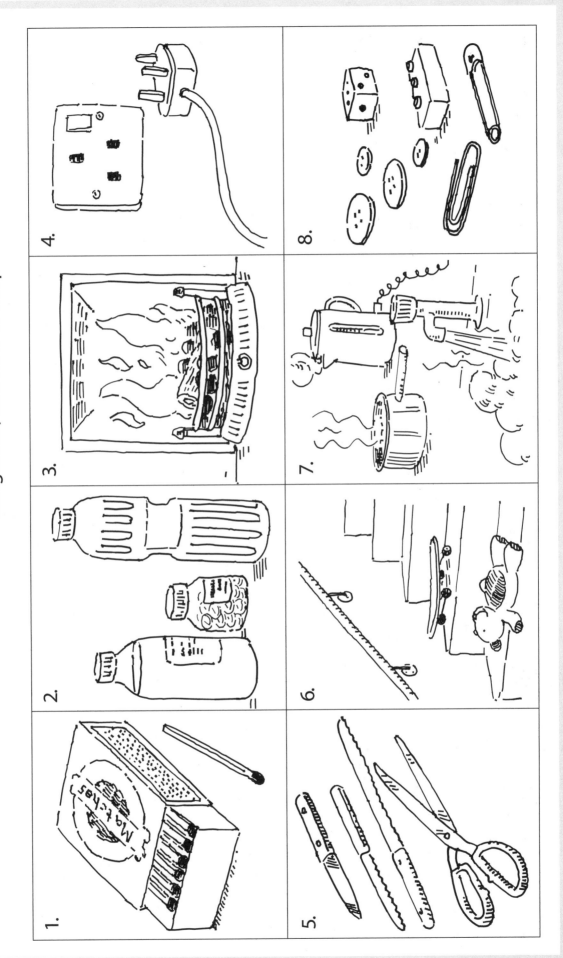

Help! I think I'm lost!

Simon was going shopping with his older sister Amy. He was excited because he had saved up his pocket money for weeks and he was longing to get to the shopping centre. It seemed such a long wait at the bus stop, but eventually the bus came and they squeezed on. They got off at the shopping centre, with Simon holding Amy's hand very tightly.

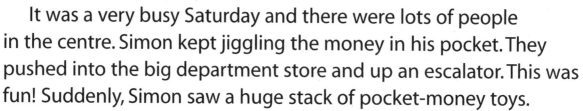

It was a very busy Saturday and there were lots of people in the centre. Simon kept jiggling the money in his pocket. They pushed into the big department store and up an escalator. This was fun! Suddenly, Simon saw a huge stack of pocket-money toys.

"Can we have a look there?" he asked Amy.

"Of course," said Amy, and over they went.

Simon started examining the colourful toys carefully. Which one was best? Just then Amy spotted her friend Mutti and they were soon happily chatting away. Simon was slowly working his way round the toy stand, completely absorbed in choosing what to buy.

Soon he found just the thing he wanted , but when he looked up to show Amy, he couldn't see her anywhere, just lots of people he didn't know! He felt afraid. He was lost!

Name   Date

People I can trust

These are the names of people I can trust:

_____

_____   _____

_____   _____

If I am worried about something, I can
speak to the people I can trust and say:

> I am afraid and I need your help...

> I want to tell you something very important...

> Please can you help me at once...?

> I am sorry to interrupt, but this is serious...

> I need to talk to you now...

■ Fill in the blank speech bubbles with your own ideas.

Emergency call!

■ Is this a real emergency?
Tick the box for yes or no and write beside it
whether you need police, fire brigade or ambulance.

Situation (There is no grown-up to help you.)	Emergency? Yes No	If yes, which emergency service?
1. You are alone with your very old grandma. She has fallen and broken her leg and can't move.	☐ ☐	_____
2. Your kitten has climbed halfway up a tree and seems unable to get down.	☐ ☐	_____
3. You see smoke and flames pouring from a house.	☐ ☐	_____
4. On a country walk you find a motorcyclist who has had an accident and is unconscious.	☐ ☐	_____
5. Your sister has cut her finger and it is bleeding a bit.	☐ ☐	_____
6. You see two people smashing a window and climbing into a house.	☐ ☐	_____

DEVELOP EFFECTIVE AND SATISFYING RELATIONSHIPS

The activities in this section focus on children:
■ reflecting on current relationships
■ meeting and developing relationships with a variety of people
■ working co-operatively, reflecting on their contributions to the group
■ voicing different opinions sensitively; being courteous
■ considering the needs of others and how their actions can have consequences for others.

TAKING TURNS

RESOURCES AND CLASSROOM ORGANIZATION

You will need: a 'new' toy or book for each group (something they have not seen before).

Children work in groups, with a final class discussion.

WHAT TO DO

Explain to the children that they are going to be thinking about sharing and taking turns. Ask: *Why is it important to share and take turns?* Children may say so that it is fair for everyone, there will be no arguing, and so on.

Divide the class into groups of about four children. Explain that each group is going to have a toy/book and everyone in the group must have a turn to look at it. Ask the children to think about how they are feeling while they are waiting, and when it is their turn. Allow about two minutes for each turn, and tell the groups when it is time to pass on the object.

After everyone has had a turn, encourage each group to discuss what their feelings were.

Now gather the class together to consider the questions: *What was it like while waiting for your turn? Were you interested, anticipating your turn with pleasure? Did you find it difficult, frustrating, boring?* Now ask: *Who managed to wait patiently for their turn?* Congratulate those people. *How did you pass the time while you were waiting?* (For example, talking quietly to a friend.) *How did it feel when it was your turn?* (Happy, pleased, excited and so on?) *What would it have been like if the group had not shared?* Perhaps there might have been arguments, some people would have felt excluded and upset because they hadn't had a turn.

Finally, ask the children: *What have you learned about sharing and taking turns?* Hopefully they will see that while it might be hard to wait for your turn, it is best for everyone in the long run. *When could you try to wait or share things in the future?* (In the class or playground, in the dinner queue, in a shop, and so on.)

NOW OR LATER

■ Children could make a decorated class statement 'In this class we like to be fair by taking turns and having a share' to display as a reminder.
■ Invite the children to make up a poem about sharing and how good it feels when a friend shares with you.

OBJECTIVES

To enable children to:
■ learn how to co-operate with others
■ consider the needs of others
■ learn how to wait their turn patiently
■ learn how to share.

CROSS-CURRICULAR LINKS

ENGLISH

Taking turns in speaking and communicating effectively in speech; poetry.

A FEELING FOR FRIENDS

RESOURCES AND CLASSROOM ORGANIZATION

You will need: a flip chart or a large sheet of paper (headed 'I can be a good friend because…'); a sheet of A4 (or larger) paper for each child with a mark on each edge about halfway along (see Figure 1); writing and drawing materials.

Children work as a class, then individually, with a final class discussion.

WHAT TO DO

Start with a class discussion about friends: *What is a friend?* (Someone who is kind to us, helps us, and likes to be with us, and so on.) *What sort of people can we be friends with?* (An adult, child, relative, someone in school, or out of school, and so on.) *What is a good friend like?* Write key words on the large sheet of paper headed 'I can be a good friend because…', for example they 'share' with us, think about 'how we are feeling', 'look after us', 'play with us'.

Then ask: *How does it feel to have a good friend?* (Good, comforting, reassuring.) *So what would it feel like if we didn't have any friends?* (Sad, lonely, unhappy.) *So can we make sure that everyone has friends?* Yes! *How could we make friends with someone who looks lonely?* (Go and talk to them! Ask them to join in our games, share our computer, and so on.)

Ask the children to do a drawing of themselves with their hands right at the edge of the paper by the marks (see Figure 2).

Explain that they should write along the top of the page 'I am a good friend because I…' and then add some words of their own or from the board to describe themselves as a friend.

In conclusion, ask the children: *What have you learned about being a good friend? How could you be a good friend to someone in the future?*

Checklist:

share	☐
am thoughtful	☐
am kind	☐
am cheerful	☐
am caring	☐
play nicely	☐
tell jokes	☐
am a good listener	☐
can do up buttons	☐

Figure 1

Figure 2

NOW OR LATER

■ The children's drawings can be put up next to each other so that they are 'holding hands', to encourage the feeling of everyone being friendly (see Figure 3).

■ Children could also consider how to cope with losing a friend, for example if they moved away, and how they could keep in touch.

Figure 3

GETTING TO KNOW YOU

RESOURCES AND CLASSROOM ORGANIZATION

You will not need any special resources for this activity.

Children work in pairs within small groups, followed by a final class discussion.

WHAT TO DO

Explain to the children that today they are going to learn about meeting new people. Ask them: *When do we meet new people?* Visitors come into school, we meet at the shops, at parties, on holiday, and so on. We introduce ourselves, or someone will introduce us, so we know their name and something about them.

Let's practise this so that we are good at remembering to introduce someone – which is the polite thing to do. Either ask the children to choose a partner whom they do not often talk to or play with (now is the chance to find out more about them), and ask these pairs to work in small groups of four to six, *or* arrange the pairs and groups yourself as you feel appropriate.

Explain to the children that they are going to take turns to introduce their partner to the group. They will have a little chat with the partner first, to find out something about them, for example where they live, if they have brothers or sisters, what their favourite game is. Give an example: 'May I introduce Manjit? She lives in the village and she has two younger brothers.' Manjit says 'Hello' and shakes hands with the group. The group say 'Hello' back. Then another person is introduced: 'This is Frazer. He has a big sister, and a cat called Suky.' Frazer says 'Hello' and shakes hands. The group says 'Hello' back. Monitor the groups and compliment children on their polite introductions.

Ask the pairs to find out one thing they have in common (to build empathy) and allow the groups to work or play together for a while to help to establish new friendships.

Now ask the children what they have learned from the introductions. *How did it feel to be introduced to the group?* (Important? Special?) *How would you feel if you met some new people who your friend knew and your friend chatted away to them, ignoring you and not introducing you?* (You might feel embarrassed, angry, left out.) *What will you be able to do in the future when meeting someone new to make yourself and them feel comfortable?*

OBJECTIVES

To enable children to:
- develop relationships with a variety of people
- consider the needs of others
- learn to be courteous

CROSS-CURRICULAR LINKS

ENGLISH

Speaking with confidence; learning about the conventions of conversation; drama – role-playing.

Now or later

■ Children could also practise introducing themselves: 'Hello, my name is… and I'm very pleased to meet you,' offering a hand to shake.
■ Children could make up their own role-play situations in which they meet new people and introduce each other – at the doctor's, at a friend's house and so on.
■ Children could find out about the ways that people of different cultures introduce themselves. Not everyone shakes hands!

My special people

Objectives

To enable children to:
■ reflect on current relationships, friends, families and carers
■ appreciate why someone is special to them
■ learn about different types of family
■ learn about the roles of the people who look after them
■ start to consider future relationships.

Cross-curricular links

English

Communicating effectively in speech and writing; formulating, clarifying and expressing ideas; making simple clear explanations of choices; writing in response to a range of stimuli, including their own experiences.

Resources and classroom organization

You will need: a copy of photocopiable page 37 for each child (this could be enlarged for younger children); writing and drawing materials.

Children work as a class, then individually.

What to do

Tell the children that they are going to think about the people that are special to them, particularly people who look after them. Ask: *Who looks after children?* to get answers about mums and/or dads, grandmas/grandpas, aunts, uncles, older brothers and sisters (and also childminders, carers, foster parents, teachers, nurses and doctors, and so on). Talk about different kinds of families. *Why are these people special to us?* (Because they look after us – feed us, keep us warm, give us clothes and so on, and love us, and we love them.) Talk about different kinds of caring. For example, going out to work and sometimes being away is caring by earning money to buy food and clothes and so on for the family. *How can we show our special people that we appreciate them?* (With thank yous, hugs and kisses, and by caring for them too, by being thoughtful about *their* needs, and by co-operating with what they ask us to do, working as a team!)

Give each child a copy of photocopiable page 37 and explain that they are going to draw a picture of themselves in the centre and their special people in the 'petals'. Explain that these can be added to later; not all the petals have to be filled in at once. Children can also write about their special people on the back of the photocopiable sheet or on a separate piece of paper.

Conclude by asking the children if this lesson has made them think in a different way about people who are special to them. *How are you going to show your special people that you really appreciate them?*

Now or later

■ Children could bring in small photographs of their special people to stick on the petals.
■ They could think about the future and about who will be special to them then – their own children, perhaps.
■ Children could collect pictures from magazines and newspapers to show different kinds of families and groups who are special to each other – members of current pop groups, rescue teams who work together, and so on.

Name   Date

Me and my special people

■ Draw yourself in the middle and your special people in the petals. Write names beside them.

The activities in this section focus on children:
- appreciating an environment where differences are respected
- interacting with a wide range of people who are different from them
- listening to and accepting other points of view
- seeing the world from other people's perspectives
- recognizing worth in others
- questioning media images and stereotypes, racism, sexism and so on
- recognizing other social groups, for example by their culture, age.

THE SAME BUT DIFFERENT

OBJECTIVES

To enable children to:
- appreciate that people have things in common and things which are different about them
- respect the physical differences between people
- recognize that each person is unique.

CROSS-CURRICULAR LINKS

SCIENCE

Finding out about the ways in which all humans are like each other and the ways in which they are different – exploring human variation; making observations and comparisons.

ENGLISH

Communicating effectively in speech, describing events, observations and experiences.

MATHS

Using purposeful contexts for measuring, collecting, recording and interpreting data using charts, tables diagrams and graphs; comparing objects using appropriate language.

RESOURCES AND CLASSROOM ORGANIZATION

You will need to prepare in advance for younger children (one for each child) a paper cut-out of four linked figures, as described below. You will also need: a cut-out of four linked figures that you have made for yourself, with the figures drawn and coloured to look identical; drawing and colouring materials for each child.

Cut an A4 sheet in half lengthways and fold one half into four. Open it up and fold it in a concertina fashion. Draw half a person on the uppermost surface. Now cut around the outline and open it up to produce four linked figures.

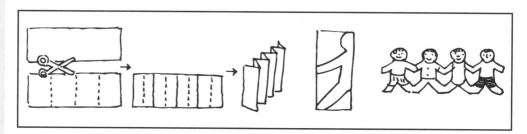

Children work in groups of four, then as a class.

WHAT TO DO

Say to the class that today they are going to think of lots of different people and consider the things about them that are the same and the things that are different. Ask: *What things are the same about everybody?* (Most people have two arms and two legs, and so on.) Then: *What differences between people can we see?* (Child/adult; boy/girl; hair/eye/skin colour; size and so on.)

Divide the children into groups of four, ideally two boys and two girls. Ask each child to look carefully at the three others in their group and then draw and colour their four cut-out people – one like themselves, and the other three like their group.

Now bring the children back together as a class with their cut-outs, and extend the discussion. Ask them if anyone in their group looked the same. *What are some of the differences between people in your group? Is anyone in the class the same as you? Do you think that anyone else in the world is exactly the same as you?* No! Even identical twins have small differences, for example one might be right-handed and the other left-handed. Luckily we are not all the same, and everyone is unique! Show them your cut-out of four *identical* people. *What would it be like if we were all exactly the same?* (Boring and confusing.) Ask: *If someone's eyes, say, are a different colour to yours, does that make the person more or less important than you?* No, everyone is different, but equally important.

Summarize by asking the children how they felt about the activity. What have they learned? That each person is unique and special.

NOW OR LATER

■ Mount the completed cut-outs onto sugar paper and display them together with children's written comments about similarities, differences and uniqueness.
■ Older or more able children could consider whether some groups of people – those with disabilities, people of an ethnic minority – are treated poorly because of their differences, and they could discuss how such prejudices could be overcome.
■ Children could collect and record data about height, foot size, hand size, arm span and so on of different members of the class, represent it as a graph and write a short commentary about the range shown.

CELEBRATING DIFFERENCES

RESOURCES AND CLASSROOM ORGANIZATION

You will need to prepare in advance (by freezing if necessary) a selection of breads from different countries, each labelled with the name and the country from which it originates (enough for small groups of children to have samples of two or three each); a large sheet of paper for class results, headed as illustrated below.

Name of bread	Country	What does it look like? (colour, shape, size)	What does it feel like? (heavy or light)	What does it smell like? (yeasty, floury, sour, herby)	What is its texture like? (open and spongy or dense)	What does it taste like? (floury, sweet, savoury)

NB Obtain parental permission for food tasting in case of allergies to nuts, gluten and so on.
   Children work as a class, then in groups, followed by a collation of class results.

WHAT TO DO

Ask the children: *Can you think of one food we can eat with lots of different things, at breakfast, lunch, tea, supper and on picnics?* (The answer is bread!) *Has anyone tasted a different kind of bread on holiday? How many kinds of bread can you think of?*

Explain that most people around the world have one or two basic breads which they make and use in different ways. These are very important for health. *We're going to find out about some of these today.*

Distribute the different breads to each group and ask the children to examine their samples and discuss and describe what each one looks like (colour, shape, size), feels like (heavy or light), smells like (floury, yeasty, herby, sour) and what texture it has (open and spongy, or thick and dense).

Let children who have permission taste the bread. Remind them to wash their hands first, and then add 'taste' to their descriptions.

Now ask each group to describe *one* particular bread to the others, and record their comments on the class sheet. Then let the groups change places, to examine each other's breads.

Explain how important our daily bread has been historically. With no supermarkets, each family had to make their own bread (some still do), even first grinding up the corn ('the daily grind'). Millers would grind corn for a fee, and bakers would bake it in a village oven. *Does anyone know anyone called Miller or Baker?*

OBJECTIVES

To enable children to:
■ respect differences between people
■ recognize worth in others
■ recognize other social groups
■ see the world from other people's perspectives.

CROSS-CURRICULAR LINKS

RELIGIOUS EDUCATION
Gaining knowledge of comparative religions.

SCIENCE:
Exploring variation in humans; learning about micro-organisms (yeast).

ENGLISH
Listening to the reactions of others, describing events, observations and experiences.

HISTORY
Investigating changes in their own lives and those of their family or adults around them.

GEOGRAPHY
Becoming aware that the world extends beyond their own locality.

Not all breads are baked in ovens. *How else could bread be cooked?* (On a 'griddle', a hot metal sheet, or even in a frying pan, as in Australian 'damper bread'.)

Finish by asking the children what they have learned. *Was it interesting finding out about breads which people from different cultures eat? Do we all take bread very much for granted?* Ask them what else they would like to find out about breads. Suggest that when they get home they could look at ingredients labels from bought breads to find out what they are made of.

NOW OR LATER

■ Children could find out where the breads came from on a world map.
■ Encourage them do some research using a variety of books, CD-ROMs or the Internet, to find out about different types of bread and link the information to other foods eaten by those cultures.
■ Other aspects of each particular culture (art, music, dance, ceremonies) can be added to their understanding of foods.
■ Children can, with help, enjoy making bread such as flowerpot loaves, soda bread or Australian damper bread, and describe their experiences of kneading, moulding and smelling freshly baked bread.
■ Visitors, perhaps parents, can be invited to demonstrate how to make a particular bread, for example chapattis, and explain its significance.
■ Children could investigate mills in different countries or visit a local working mill, and find out about different types of strong bread flours, and from which grain or seed they come.
■ In science children can investigate the micro-organism yeast, and how it 'bubbles' in warm sugar water, to provide the rise in 'leavened' bread.

LET'S BE FAIR

OBJECTIVES

To enable children to:
■ consider the principle of fairness and relate it to themselves and others
■ understand why fairness is important
■ see the world from other people's perspectives.

CROSS-CURRICULAR LINKS

ENGLISH

Formulating, clarifying and expressing ideas; describing events, observations and experiences; reading for information; extended writing.

ICT

Using equipment to carry out a variety of functions.

RESOURCES AND CLASSROOM ORGANIZATION

You will need: a copy of photocopiable page 41 and scissors for each pair; an exercise book or paper for each child; writing materials.

Children work in pairs and individually, followed by a brief class discussion.

WHAT TO DO

Introduce the activity by explaining that the children are going to think about being fair and whether this is important in our everyday lives.

Divide the class into pairs, and give the children time to discuss the statements on photocopiable page 41, cut them out and sort them into 'fair' and 'unfair' piles.

Now discuss their decisions as a class. Ask them: *What do we mean by being fair?* It nearly always means being equal, but also can depend on someone's needs (such as an older child going to bed later). *Is it important to try and be fair?* (Yes, because everyone has a right to be treated fairly.) *What does it feel like when things are not fair?* (You feel resentful, frustrated, jealous, envious.)

For each of the given scenarios, ask the pairs to explain what the opposite one would be. For example, for scenario 2 it might be Mum unfairly giving only four sweets to one child. Finally, ask the children to write down their own examples under the headings 'fair' and 'unfair'.

Round off by asking children what they feel about fairness and unfairness. Does it sometimes need to be discussed carefully? Will this affect their actions in the future?

NOW OR LATER

■ Children could write their own stories on the computer about an unfair situation which is then resolved.
■ More able children could look through (suitable) newspapers to find stories of situations they consider to be unfair, then discuss how they feel about them.

Let's be fair

1. Class one always go into dinner first and class two always wait until later.

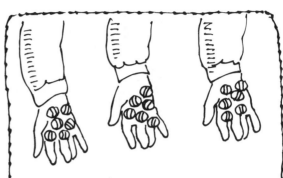

2. Mum shared out the sweets so that each child had six.

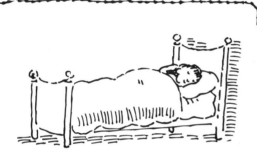

3. Sunhil was two years older than Preetpal and was allowed to go to bed later.

4. Jessica and Xander had been on the computer all morning and would not let Suki and Jacob have their turn.

5. Samba and Laura helped themselves to all the new paper so there was none left for the rest of the class.

6. Mrs Lloyd started a new maths club at school and said that anyone could join.

■ Cut out the boxes and sort them into two piles, one for **fair** and one for **unfair**. Talk about why you have put each box where it is.

The activities in this section focus on children:
- facing challenges in a supportive environment
- taking responsibility for themselves, including their behaviour and their own learning
- being involved in the development and implementation of an anti-bullying policy
- looking ahead, to growing older
- developing trustworthiness and reliability.

NO BULLYING ALLOWED

OBJECTIVES

To enable children to:
- face challenges in a supportive environment
- take responsibility for their own behaviour
- be involved in the development and implementation of an anti-bullying policy

CROSS-CURRICULAR LINKS

ENGLISH

Communicating effectively in speech and writing; formulating, clarifying and expressing ideas; predicting outcomes and discussing possibilities.

DESIGN & TECHNOLOGY

Using design skills; making freehand drawings; considering their design ideas to identify strengths and weaknesses.

RESOURCES AND CLASSROOM ORGANIZATION

You will need: three large sheets of paper headed (1) 'Nice ways to behave', (2) 'Unkind ways to behave', (3) 'What we can do about bullying'; sheets of poster paper (two per group); colouring and art materials.

Children work as a class, then in pairs or groups, with a final class discussion.

WHAT TO DO

Say to the children: *Today we are going to think a lot about ways we behave towards each other. We're going to talk about what are nice and unkind ways of behaving.*

First of all, let's think about nice behaviour. What can we do to be nice to each other? (Smile, say nice things, praise and help people, be friendly, don't deliberately bump into other people, and so on.) List these on sheet 1. *How do we feel when people behave like this to us?* (Happy, encouraged, good about ourselves, likely to be nice to someone else.) Write these on sheet 1 under 'We feel…'

Nice ways to behave ✓
Open doors for people. Helping
Say "hello"
Smile at someone
Sharing. Playing

We feel….
Happy. Good about ourselves

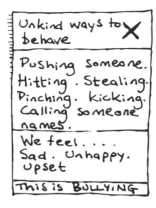
Unkind ways to behave ✗
Pushing someone.
Hitting. Stealing.
Pinching. kicking.
Calling someone names.

We feel….
Sad. Unhappy. upset

THIS IS BULLYING

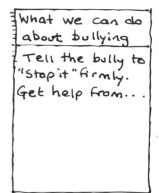
What we can do about bullying
Tell the bully to "stop it" firmly.
Get help from…

Now ask for examples of 'unkind' behaviour, for example saying unkind things, jeering, teasing, name calling, taking things without permission, hitting, kicking, and so on. List these on sheet 2, together with 'We feel…' sad, bewildered, upset, worried, frightened, hurt. Ask the class to vote on which way they would like people to behave towards them. No contest! Sheet 1 should get unanimous acclaim.

So why do people sometimes behave the other way? They might be feeling a bit 'grumpy' (and we all have days when we feel fed up), but if someone does these things to someone else for more than a very short time, we call it bullying behaviour. Write this on the bottom of sheet 2. *Why do you think some people bully other people?* They may be very unhappy, or angry about something, so they may need help too, to solve their problems and not to 'take it out' on someone else.

42

Explain the school anti-bullying policy, and that bullying is *not* tolerated, either in the class, at playtime or on the way home. *So what can we do to make sure that bullying does not happen, and everyone can feel 'safe'?* Ask for answers and write them on sheet 3. Tell the children: *We can stick up for ourselves or someone being bullied at once, look the bully in the eye and tell him or her to stop it. Get help from other children, or a teacher or supervisor…* These ideas can be added to as the need arises, and turned into a list of 'Class rules'.

Now ask the children to work in pairs or small groups and design and colour two posters – one showing how people like to be treated, the other an 'anti-bullies' one.

Round off the session by encouraging the children to show their posters to others in the class and to explain how they felt while they were making them. Remind the class of who individuals can go to if they want to tell an adult something 'in confidence'. Reinforce the 'zero tolerance' to bullies. Explain that action will be taken against bullies, but they will also be given help to enable them to behave better.

NOW OR LATER

■ Hold a competition for the best poster design. The winning poster could be reproduced for display all around the school.

■ Children could do a survey to find out how everyone at school feels about bullying. They could produce a book about the results, and give a 'talk' to other classes about their findings.

■ Hold an anti-bullying assembly. The class could tell everyone what they feel about bullying and show their posters. It would be very helpful if the headteacher could then reinforce the messages personally.

BORROWING AND LENDING

RESOURCES AND CLASSROOM ORGANIZATION

You will need: some of the children's own possessions – small objects such as pencils, felt-tipped pens, pencil sharpeners, erasers and so on to 'lend and borrow'.

Children work in pairs and in small groups of four, then end with a class discussion.

WHAT TO DO

Ask two children to come out to the front of the class, one of them bringing a small object such as a pencil sharpener, which they often lend one another. Explain to the class: *We are going to think carefully about lending and borrowing things, and how we feel about this.*

Ask the two children to demonstrate the *polite* way to ask to borrow something, and to lend it with good grace, talking about the meaning of the words 'lend' and 'borrow', compared with 'give' and 'take'. When we *borrow* something, our responsibilities are to remember who we borrowed it from, and to give it back in good

OBJECTIVES

To enable children to:
■ take responsibility for themselves
■ become trustworthy and reliable
■ appreciate and take care of their own and others' possessions
■ practise being assertive

CROSS-CURRICULAR LINKS

ENGLISH
Responding appropriately to others; predicting outcomes and discussing possibilities; writing; drama – role-playing.

condition. In other words, we look after it, and say thank you and be appreciative. When we *lend* something, we expect to get it back quite soon. If we don't, we can ask for it politely. (If the child is at school, and it isn't returned, the teacher may be able to help.)

When we borrow something we show that we are *reliable*, so our friend will trust us again. Some things might be very special to us, and we don't want to lend them to anybody, so we *can* (politely) refuse – this is our right. Now let the two children demonstrate this.

Divide the class into small groups of four. One pair should role-play lending and borrowing small items, politely, allowing (or refusing) to lend them, and asking for them back firmly, or assertively. The observers comment on their skills. Pairs then swap over.

Now gather the class back together to discuss what they have learned. Ask them to tell you the meanings of 'lend', 'borrow', 'trust' and 'reliable'. Ask: *What must we do if we borrow something?* and *What does it feel like if we lend something and don't get it back, or it comes back broken?* Let this lead on to exploring the importance of being able to trust people and rely on them, and the importance of respecting property – our own, and other people's. If you have borrowed something and it gets broken, you should apologize, and have it mended or replaced if possible.

NOW OR LATER

■ Children could write down the new words they have learned, with their definitions underneath.

■ Can the children think of examples of borrowing and lending? (Such as using a library, renting a house, hiring tools.)

■ Children could write a short story involving lending and borrowing. This could feature someone refusing to lend something because the person who borrowed an item last time didn't give it back, or broke it.

WHERE AM I GROWING TO?

OBJECTIVES

To enable children to:
■ look ahead to growing older with confidence
■ start to understand the human life cycle
■ start to appreciate the needs of people of different ages.

CROSS-CURRICULAR LINKS

ENGLISH

Listening; understanding; predicting outcomes; making clear, simple explanations of choices.

SCIENCE

Understanding health and growth.

RESOURCES AND CLASSROOM ORGANIZATION

You will need: a copy of photocopiable page 46 and scissors for each child; glue; exercise book or a plain sheet of paper for each child; board or flip chart.

Children work as a class, then in pairs or small groups, with a final class discussion.

WHAT TO DO

Start by talking to the whole class about families and carers. Ask: *Who has older brothers and sisters? How old are they? Who in your family is even older than this?* (Parents, uncles/aunts, grandparents and so on.) Thus reinforce the sequence of growth, that we *all* start out as babies, become toddlers, older children, teenagers, adults and older adults (and eventually, we die).

Now ask the children: *What are you looking forward to being able to do when you are older?* As they respond, help them to get an idea of what age they will be able to do certain things, for example drive a car at 17 years old. As they grow up they will be able to take more responsibility for themselves, and may eventually be responsible for other people if they choose to have a family or look after their own parents when they get very old, or become a teacher or a carer. Talk about the needs and responsibilities of each life stage. Reassure them that they will get a lot of help when growing up, and be given time to learn new skills and training to take on new responsibilities.

Give each child a copy of photocopiable page 46 to cut out the figures and ask pairs or small groups to sort them into the right order. (The intended sequence is e, c, f, h, b, g, d, a.) When you have checked them, the children can stick them onto their sheet or in their book. If appropriate, write words on the board to describe the stages for the children to copy underneath the figures: baby, toddler, young child, older child, teenager, young adult, older adult, old adult.

Conclude by asking the children how they felt about doing this activity and what they have found out that they didn't know before. How do they feel about their present stage of life?

NOW OR LATER

■ Enlarge the photocopiable sheet for the children to paint the figures. They could be displayed in sequence on a noticeboard. The children could then bring in pictures from magazines to put up next to each life stage, and write about their feelings at each stage.

■ Invited parents or friends could talk about the different life stages and their personal experiences, for example an elderly person could show a sequence of photographs of himself (or herself) from birth to present day.

■ Children could collect photographs from magazines (or from computer CDs) of famous people as babies. 'From small acorns do mighty oak trees grow!'

WHAT WOULD YOU DO?

RESOURCES AND CLASSROOM ORGANIZATION

You will need: a copy of photocopiable page 47 for each pair; writing materials.

After an introductory whole-class discussion, children work in pairs, followed by a final class discussion.

WHAT TO DO

Talk to the children about making choices and deciding what to do – that is, making decisions. When something unusual happens, we need to stop and think carefully about what would be the right thing to do. Explain that we can practise this by thinking ahead.

Give out copies of photocopiable page 47, one between two. Read it through as a class, then ask the children to discuss their choices, in pairs, and tick their chosen boxes. Then come back together again.

Ask the class to talk about their decisions, so that the children can explain the reasons why they made their particular choices. Talk about being sensible, being safe, being responsible for themselves, being kind and thoughtful, getting help, not panicking, being honest, and not involving the teacher with every tiny incident!

Ask: *What did you feel about this activity? What have you learned that you might be able to use in the future? What other things might we have to make choices about?*

NOW OR LATER

■ Children could make up their own situations to swap with others and discuss the answers.

■ They could act out a given situation showing the alternatives and ask the audience to choose the most appropriate response.

■ Children could write their own story called 'Decision time', in which the main character has an important choice to make.

■ Older children could lead on to a discussion about future choices adults have to make in life, such as what job to do, where to live, whether to have children, and so on.

OBJECTIVES

To enable children to:
■ learn how to make sensible choices and decisions
■ face challenges in a supportive environment
■ take responsibility for themselves, including their behaviour and their own learning
■ become trustworthy and reliable.

CROSS-CURRICULAR LINKS

ENGLISH

Predicting outcomes and discussing possibilities; making simple, clear explanations of choices; drama; extended writing.

Where am I growing to?

■ Cut around the figures and put them in order of age, starting with the youngest.

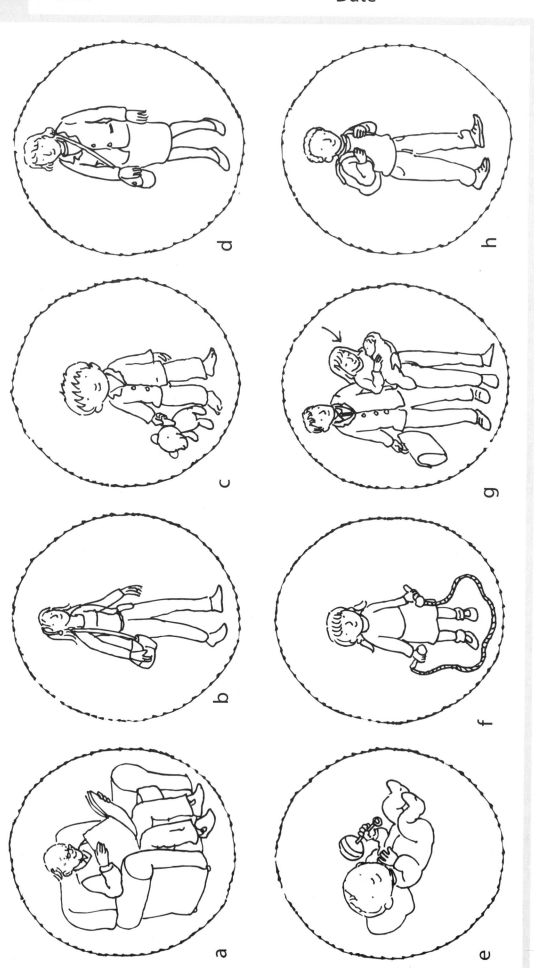

Ready to go! IDEAS FOR PSHE

What would you do?

■ Discuss the choices and then tick the right box.

1. You accidentally knock over an ornament at home and it breaks.	Mend it and pretend nothing happened. ☐ Go and say sorry straight away. ☐ Walk away. Say you know nothing about it. ☐
2. Someone in your class is rude to you.	Be rude back to them. ☐ Say calmly, "Don't be rude," and walk away. ☐ Shout, "She/he was rude to me!" ☐
3. A new child is standing alone in the playground.	Ask them to join in a game. ☐ Take no notice of them. ☐ Point at them and whisper to your friend. ☐
4. It's time for games but you can't find your PE kit.	Panic. Shout, "I can't find my PE kit!" ☐ Look carefully on the floor or on other pegs. 'Borrow' someone else's kit. ☐
5. At break a girl has fallen and can't get up.	Phone for an ambulance! ☐ Be careful not to trip over her when playing. Tell someone on dinner duty. ☐
6. You have left tonight's homework sheet at school.	Say that you didn't have any homework. ☐ Apologize to the teacher the next day. ☐ Say to the teacher that you weren't given a sheet. ☐
7. Someone dares you to do something naughty.	Say, "That would be a silly thing to do." ☐ Go and do the naughty thing. ☐ Ask a friend to go with you to do it. ☐

The activities in this section focus on children:
- taking a responsible role in school
- taking part in the decision-making process of the school
- working with their local community and understanding how it functions
- being involved with an environmental project, observing their local surroundings and making improvements
- caring for animals and plants
- understanding shops and services, and how these are paid for.

OUR CLASS RULES, OK!

OBJECTIVES

To enable children to:
- take a responsible role in school
- take part in the decision-making process of the school
- understand the need for rules.

CROSS-CURRICULAR LINKS

ENGLISH

Formulating, clarifying and expressing ideas; knowing the conventions of discussion, for example taking turns in speaking, expressing themselves confidently and clearly.

ICT

Using equipment for a variety of purposes.

ART

Communicating meaning in a visual form.

RESOURCES AND CLASSROOM ORGANIZATION

You will need: a copy of your school rules (these could be on an OHT); flip chart; paper; writing and colouring materials.

Children work as a class, followed by an individual activity and a final class discussion.

WHAT TO DO

Explain to the children that in order for everyone to work and play happily, they are going to work out their own class rules. Start by asking: *Can anyone tell me any of the school's rules?* As each rule is suggested, ask the children for the reason for the rule, for example 'Don't run' is for safety. Discuss all the school rules, then ask: *So what do we mean by a rule?* (A rule tells us something that we must or must not do.) *Why do we have rules?* (Because people might otherwise not be considerate; we need rules to ensure that everyone behaves sensibly.)

Now turn to considering rules for the class. Explain that you want to have as few rules as possible, so that they will be easy to remember and keep to. Ask the children for suggestions, writing each one on the flip chart. Help them to amalgamate the rules to make a few simple ones. For example, 'No pushing or shoving' and 'No pinching or poking' could become 'We treat everyone with respect'. Discuss in detail the reason(s) for each one and ask the children to agree to obey it, so that the class 'owns' its own rules.

Suggestions might include:
- We will help each other to work.
- We will listen when the teacher is talking.
- We will look after our own and other people's property.

Now write a final list of rules on another page of the flip chart and display it prominently in the classroom. The children can then produce their own lists on the computer. Ask them to 'sign' their name at the bottom of a printed copy to agree to respect the rules. They can then decorate the border and fasten the list to the inside of their desk lids, or on the front of a regularly used folder.

Round off the activity by asking the children what they have learned about rules. *What might happen if there were no rules?* Can they remember the new class rules? How will they apply them in the future? *What should happen to people who don't keep to the rules?*

NOW OR LATER

■ Children could paint pictures to illustrate each of their class rules and/or the school rules, for display.
■ Encourage the children to find out about local rules (by-laws), such as parking restrictions, and what happens if you break them!
■ Children could collect examples of other classes' 'rules' to look at and compare with their own. They could review their class rules at the beginning and end of each term to assess how effective they have been and if any changes are necessary.

PAMPER A PET

RESOURCES AND CLASSROOM ORGANIZATION

You will need: a class/school pet or pets, or a visitor with pets; a copy of photocopiable page 54 and scissors for each child; glue; plain sheets of paper; writing materials.

Children work both as a class and individually.

WHAT TO DO

If the children are not already familiar with the pet, begin by introducing it to the class. Let the children ask you (if it is a class pet) or the owner questions about what the pet's needs are, and discuss how it has to be looked after. Talk about the advantages and disadvantages of having a pet.

Give out copies of photocopiable page 54 and explain to the children what they have to do:
■ They choose one of the five pets shown and cut out its picture.
■ For each of the categories (food, exercise, home and so on) they choose the right box or boxes to cut out.
■ Finally, they stick all their chosen boxes next to one another under the heading 'Pamper a pet'.
■ Older or more able children can then write a description of the pet and its needs, adding any special considerations not covered by the photocopiable sheet.

Once the photocopiable sheets have been completed, bring the class back together to talk about their chosen pets and compare their needs with human needs – air, food, drink, exercise, home, company, keeping clean, doctor (vet) and so on.

Conclude by asking the children how they felt about meeting a real pet. Do they think pets are easy to look after or will they need a lot of time, care and attention every day (week, month, year)? *What would happen to the pet without this care?*

Not everyone is able to keep a pet at home, but we can all help to care for animals in the wild. How can we do this? By, for example, creating and looking after wildlife habitats (homes) for all sorts of animals (see the next activity 'Let's look around us'), by setting up bird-feeders and growing plants (like buddleia) that butterflies like.

NOW OR LATER

■ Children could find out more about many different pets – stick insects, spiders, snakes, toads, fish and so on – bringing in pictures and books, and items that such pets would need.

■ Ask the children to design an 'ideal' imaginative home for a chosen pet. It could then be constructed and given a model pet inhabitant.

■ Children with pets could paint a portrait of their pet and add interesting illustrative details.

■ Arrange to visit a pet shop, veterinary surgery, zoo or farm and ask prepared questions about how the animals are cared for.

LET'S LOOK AROUND US

OBJECTIVES

To enable children to:
■ take a responsible role in school
■ take part in the decision-making process of the school
■ learn to appreciate the importance of a good environment
■ be involved with an environmental project, observing their local surroundings and making improvements.

CROSS-CURRICULAR LINKS

ENGLISH
Writing in response to experiences; discussing possibilities; making clear explanations of choices.

MATHS
Using purposeful contexts for measuring.

SCIENCE
Recognizing ways to protect living things and the environment.

DESIGN & TECHNOLOGY
Using designing skills, making freehand drawings.

GEOGRAPHY
Studying the locality, including quality of the environment and how it could be improved.

ICT
Using equipment for a variety of functions.

HISTORY
Investigating changes and why events happened.

RESOURCES AND CLASSROOM ORGANIZATION

You will need: permission to look for school areas needing improvement; a copy of photocopiable page 55 and a clipboard for each child; if possible, extra adults to help; board or flip chart; drawing paper (large or small sheets); ideally, a budget to make improvements to classroom/school grounds; map of the school grounds (optional); tape-measures (optional); writing and drawing materials.

Children work as a class, then in groups outside, ending with a class discussion.

WHAT TO DO

Ask the children to look around them and tell you about all the things they like about their classroom – from 'big windows' to 'attractive displays and pictures'. Now ask: *Is there anything you would like to make better?* (Fresh paint on the walls, a new carpet, more storage, rearrangement of the tables, for example.) Explain that the school has only a limited amount of money, but if they could have just one thing, what would this be?

Point out that they have actually been talking about their 'environment', in other words, their surroundings. Now they are going to look at the outside environment, the school grounds.

Ask the children to think about and tell you what sorts of things they would like to be able to do in the school grounds. These could be noted on the board as:

■ Active things – running about, playing games, climbing on frames, skipping
■ Quiet things – sitting chatting to friends, enjoying flowers, playing with small toys, sitting in the shade
■ Exploring things – observing wildlife, the first snowdrops or butterflies, observing seasonal changes on a nature trail, growing flowers, herbs and vegetables.

Explain that they are going to check the school grounds to see in which areas they could do these activities. What other things in the 'outside environment' could they check on to see if they could be improved?

Now give out the clipboards with photocopiable page 55, and divide the children into small groups, each with an adult helper if possible. Either allow each group to cover all the activities, or allocate a different activity to each group (for example, commenting on the 'quiet' areas or taking measurements for drawing a plan to scale later). Warn the children to stay with their group and keep clear of any identified danger areas. Move around the groups helping them with their tasks.

Back in the classroom, ask each group to report their findings. These could be summarized on a large map of the school grounds, with drawings of how things are now, and how they might be improved. Discuss their priorities and how these might be achieved – 'sponsor a shrub', 'be a litter picker', and so on. Enable children to carry out any improvements which are possible. Perhaps their plans could be presented to the school PTA for consideration.

Finally, ask the children how they felt about the activity. What have they learned about their environment? Will this help them to appreciate it better in the future? What more could they do?

Now or later

■ Children could design a 'fantasy' ideal classroom or school.

■ Help the children to devise a questionnaire on the computer to ask other classes their opinions about their classroom and/or the school grounds, to help with their planning.

■ Ask the children to write up the project, including every stage from assessment and planning to completion.

■ The project could be used as an assembly or open day, with parents invited to an opening ceremony for the improved grounds.

■ Children could devise a checklist and a rota for monitoring the improvements in the grounds and report back to a teacher – for example, are the new litter bins being used?

■ Suggest that the children go out into the wider environment (such as a local park) with an adult, to carry out the same process of assessment and planning, sending their results to the local council for comment.

■ Children could find out about the history of their school and what the grounds used to look like, ten, twenty, fifty or a hundred years ago.

BEFRIEND A SHOPKEEPER

RESOURCES AND CLASSROOM ORGANIZATION

You will need: to find a shopkeeper from a local general store, willing to talk to the children at the school, then happy for you to arrange a class or small group visit to the shop; a large photograph or picture of the shop; a copy of photocopiable page 56 for each child; board or flip chart; writing and drawing materials.

The activity is in four parts: a class discussion, a visit from the shopkeeper, a visit to the shop by the children and a final discussion.

WHAT TO DO

Show the class the picture of the shop and ask: *Does anyone recognize this? Where is it? What can we buy in our local shop? How useful is it having a shop nearby?* We can easily pop in to the friendly local shop instead of having to make a long journey to the main shops or supermarket (not everyone is able to make such a long journey).

OBJECTIVES

To enable children to:
■ understand the functioning of their local community
■ understand shops and services
■ appreciate the roles of different people in society
■ learn to interact with different people.

CROSS-CURRICULAR LINKS

ENGLISH
Communicating effectively in speech and writing; listening, understanding and responding appropriately to others; writing in response to experiences and classroom activities.

GEOGRAPHY
Studying a locality, including shops.

MATHS
Solving problems with whole numbers, including situations involving money.

ART
Recording what has been observed.

Explain that the local shopkeeper might be able to come in to answer any questions they would like to ask. *What questions could we ask him or her?* Help them formulate a list, writing the questions on the board:

■ What do you *sell* in your shop?
■ What do people *buy* most of?
■ Where do the *supplies* for the shop come from?
■ How do you *order* supplies?
■ How many people visit your shop every day?
■ Do children always behave well in your shop?
■ What are the opening times of the shop?

Check that the children understand the meaning of the words in italic. As a class, plan a letter of invitation, deciding who is to meet and escort the shopkeeper to their classroom, and thank him or her afterwards.

During the visit, individual children can read out the questions in turn. The shopkeeper might end with some questions of his or her own (for example, 'What do you like best about my shop?') and provide ideas on how children can help local shopkeepers.

If appropriate, the class or groups of children can visit the shop at a later date, each child taking their photocopiable sheet and a pencil. During the visit, ask them to note prices and extra services such as if there is a post office or dry-cleaning collection, or whether there is parking space.

After the visit discuss the importance of local shops. *What would it be like if our local shop closed?* (It would be inconvenient, there would be nowhere to meet people, buy comics, and so on.) *Do you think it is easy running a shop?* (No, there are lots of things to do and long hours to work.) *So how can we help our local shopkeeper?* (By being well behaved, considerate and by using the shop as much as possible – 'Use it or lose it'!)

Finish the activity by encouraging the children to reflect on what they have learned, and to write an illustrated 'thank you' letter to the shopkeeper.

NOW OR LATER

■ Children could set up a 'shop' using toy money in a corner of the classroom.
■ Children could paint pictures of the shopkeeper and the outside (or inside) of the shop for display – perhaps in the shop itself.
■ Children could write a story based on 'A day in the life of a local shopkeeper'.
■ Children could count out the correct money for each price written on photocopiable page 56. This could be followed up with a maths exercise about working out the right change.

THE COMMUNITY I BELONG TO

RESOURCES AND CLASSROOM ORGANIZATION

You will need as many as possible of the following: a local map; a county map; a globe; a picture of the solar system and the universe; an atlas; two large sheets of paper headed (1) 'Our school community' and (2) 'Our local community'; a copy of photocopiable page 57 for each child; plain paper; writing and colouring materials.

Children work as a class, then individually, and have a final class discussion.

WHAT TO DO

Start the activity by asking the children where they live. Part of their answer will include the name of their local town or village. Ask: *Who knows which county we live in? Which country are we living in?*

Help the children identify where they are on the local map and the map of the whole country. Show them the globe and ask: *Who can find where we are in the world on this globe?* Then show the children that the world is part of the solar system which in turn belongs to the universe. Next, show them how to come back down again from universe to solar system, to world, to Europe, to country, to county, to town/village.

Continue: *Now let's think about where we belong. We all belong to a community, which means a group of people who live near one another and meet together to live, work and play. Which groups do you belong to in the community?* (Family, friends, school, school groups/clubs, perhaps church, community centre, maybe Rainbows or Beavers of the Guide and Scout Association.)

Explain that in a community everyone depends on each other for different things. Each person living in the community is called a citizen. Ask: *Who do we need in our school community?* (Teachers, children, secretaries, cleaners, cooks, supervisors, a caretaker, and so on.) List these on sheet 1. *Who do we need in our town/village community?* (Shopkeepers, bankers, doctors, nurses, dentists, librarians, and so on.) List these on sheet 2.

So we all look after one another by providing different services or things to buy. Write some examples on the sheet beside each person, for example 'Caretaker… looks after our school heating, security…' Explain that this interdependency can involve the whole country, for example food may come from other places, and indeed the whole world, as we get many things from other countries.

Give each child a copy of photocopiable page 57 and ask them (using the local maps, county maps, atlases and the globe for reference) to mark their own town or village, colour in their county and their country (first in Europe, then in the world), and write in the box the communities and the groups to which they belong. Ask the children to consider how they are involved with and how they support their local community – in other words, how they are good citizens!

NOW OR LATER

■ Children could take part in an event to help the local community – planting flowers, for example, or visiting a day centre to read poems or stories.
■ Invite the children to 'show and tell' about groups they belong to such as Brownies/Beavers or St John's Ambulance, bringing in their uniform, badges and so on.
■ Following a class discussion, the children could write about what it would be like to live in a very isolated community with only a few people, for example in the Australian outback (using the 'radio' school and doctor) or on a remote island off the coast of Scotland.

OBJECTIVES

To enable children to:
■ work with their local community and understand how it functions
■ understand the importance of community and of becoming a good citizen
■ feel involved with and part of their local community
■ consider the wider communities of their country and the world.

CROSS-CURRICULAR LINKS

ENGLISH
Listening with understanding.

GEOGRAPHY
Studying the locality including human features; becoming aware that the world extends beyond their own locality.

Ready to go! **IDEAS FOR PSHE**

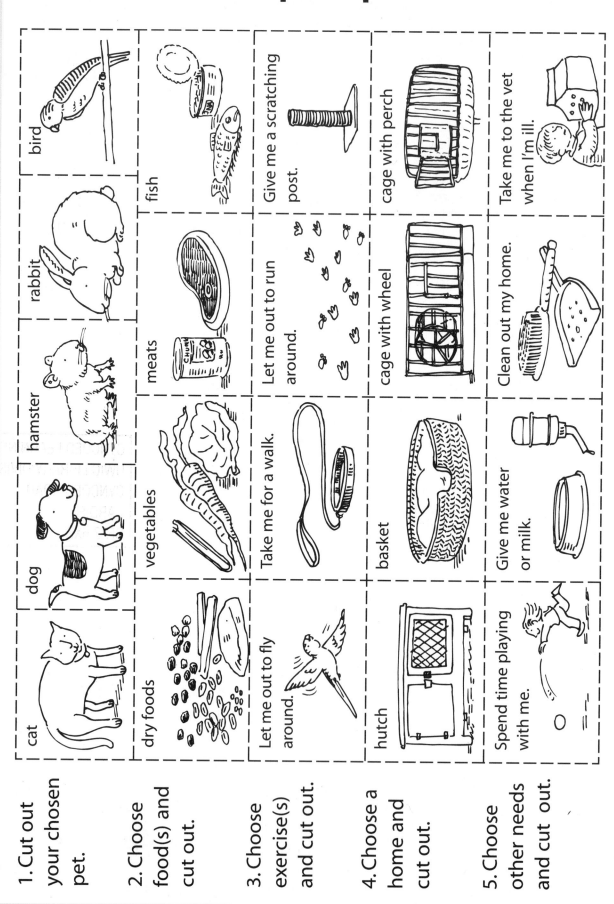

Pamper a pet

Name

Date

1. Cut out your chosen pet.

bird rabbit hamster dog cat

2. Choose food(s) and cut out.

fish meats vegetables dry foods

3. Choose exercise(s) and cut out.

Give me a scratching post. Let me out to run around. Take me for a walk. Let me out to fly around.

4. Choose a home and cut out.

cage with perch cage with wheel basket hutch

5. Choose other needs and cut out.

Take me to the vet when I'm ill. Clean out my home. Give me water or milk. Spend time playing with me.

Name   Date

 # School grounds survey

■ Are there any areas for being active (playgrounds, field, climbing frame, etc)?

Good points:

Could be improved by:

■ Are there any areas for being quiet (seats, quiet corners)?

Good points:

Could be improved by:

■ Are there any areas for exploring wildlife (shrubs, trees, nature trail, pond)?

Good points:

Could be improved by:

■ Look at the school buildings (walls, paintwork, doors).

Good points:

Could be improved by:

Shop visit worksheet

Name of the shop: _____

Name of the shopkeeper(s): _____

Opening times: _____

My favourite things about the shop:

_____

_____

■ Find out the price of:

Six eggs 	A tin of baked beans 
A loaf of bread 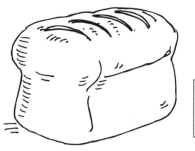	Your favourite sweets 
A newspaper 	A carton of milk 

Ready to go! IDEAS FOR PSHE

Name _____   Date _____

I belong to the world community!

1. Put a dot where your village/town is.

2. Colour in your county in the United Kingdom.

3. Colour in your country in Europe.

4. Colour in your country in the world.

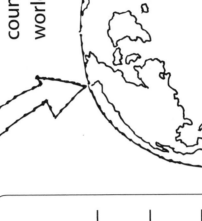

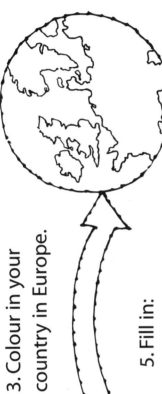

5. Fill in:

I belong to these communities:
Village/town _____

County _____

Country _____

and these groups:
School _____

Others _____

The activities in this section focus on children:
■ making choices about their future
■ being involved in assessing their work and setting targets for improvement
■ gaining more understanding of the world of work
■ recognizing what they are good at and being able to make choices
■ interviewing adults, talking to adults and listening to adult experiences
■ knowing it's OK to make mistakes, and being able to learn from them.

HAVEN'T I DONE WELL!

OBJECTIVES

To enable children to:
■ be involved in assessing their work and setting targets for improvement
■ develop key skills relevant to learning and work
■ recognize what they are good at
■ know that it's OK to make mistakes, and to learn from them.

CROSS-CURRICULAR LINKS

ENGLISH
Listening with understanding; discussing possibilities.

ART
Recording what has been observed.

RESOURCES AND CLASSROOM ORGANIZATION

This activity would ideally be done at the end of a term or year. You will need: a copy of photocopiable page 61 for each child; paper; writing and drawing materials.

Children work as a class, followed by individual work and teacher–pupil one-to-one work.

WHAT TO DO

Explain to the children that they are going to remind themselves of all their achievements this term/year.

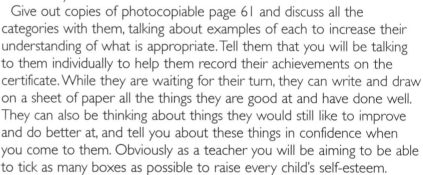

Give out copies of photocopiable page 61 and discuss all the categories with them, talking about examples of each to increase their understanding of what is appropriate. Tell them that you will be talking to them individually to help them record their achievements on the certificate. While they are waiting for their turn, they can write and draw on a sheet of paper all the things they are good at and have done well. They can also be thinking about things they would still like to improve and do better at, and tell you about these things in confidence when you come to them. Obviously as a teacher you will be aiming to be able to tick as many boxes as possible to raise every child's self-esteem.

When everyone has completed a certificate, gather the class together and ask them if they have found out something about themselves they hadn't realized before. Then invite each child to tell everyone about one achievement of which they are proud. After each child has spoken, encourage the rest of the class to applaud the achievement.

Finally, praise the children for what they have achieved as a class and ask them if they would like to set themselves any short or long term goals. Would they like to make a 'Class certificate of achievement'? What would they record on it?

NOW OR LATER

■ Certificates could be presented during a special ceremony or assembly and/or displayed or taken home. (A photocopy could be kept for school records.)
■ This activity could lead on to the more formal assessment linked to target-setting in the school.
■ Children could draw or paint a picture of themselves and add a written statement about their achievements, such as 'I am especially proud of…' or 'I am going to try harder at…', if they wish.
■ This PSHE assessment could become a regular event, for example at the end of every half-term or term. Children could keep their certificates in a folder and monitor their own and the class's progress.

NOBODY'S PERFECT!

RESOURCES AND CLASSROOM ORGANIZATION

You will need: a copy of photocopiable page 62 for each pair of children; if possible, the photocopiable short stories on an OHT to be projected.

Children have a class discussion with optional writing afterwards.

WHAT TO DO

Start by telling the children about a mistake you made recently and how it was put right. This helps them to see that 'everyone makes mistakes'.

Explain that they are going to consider the short stories on the photocopiable sheet, and give these out. Project the OHT and consider each story as a class. For each situation, read out the story with the children, then discuss who the child in the story should apologize to and what could be done to make amends. Ask why they think the mistake was made, and what could be done to prevent a similar thing happening again.

Some suggestions for discussion are:
■ Matthew – apologizes to teacher and brings the reading book the next day. Reason: forgetfulness. Solution: make a checklist of things to take to school; stop and think before you leave!
■ Sabrina – apologizes to teacher, does maths from correct page (possibly at break). Reason: perhaps not listening carefully enough. Solution: listen to the teacher, concentrate and check on what has to be done.
■ Sukhpal – apologizes to teacher. Could cut out the page and stick it in the right way up. Reason: tiredness. Solution: if possible, don't stay up late on school days.
■ Janine – apologizes to friend, buys her a new felt-tipped pen. Reason: not thinking. Solution: always take special care when you borrow someone else's things.
■ Joe – apologizes to parents/carers. Could help to mend or pay for the table leg to be mended. Reason: excited, rushing around. Solution: try to keep calm when having a friend round to play; don't run indoors.
■ Maisy – apologizes to Mum/Dad/carer who will have to fetch the sweatshirt from the museum. Reason: forgetfulness. Solution: when on a trip, try to remember all your belongings.

Summarize by reminding the children that *everyone* makes mistakes. Sometimes we can work out why, but there isn't always an obvious reason – it's just that we are human! We have to accept that we have made a mistake, own up and apologize. Try not to get upset – 'it's no use crying over spilt milk!' People will usually understand. For example, when doing some new work at school, teachers don't expect that everyone will do it exactly right the first time, and only expect that you will try to do your best. So it is very important not to let the fear of making a mistake stop you from trying!

Ask the children: *How might you feel when you have made a mistake?* (Perhaps a bit embarrassed.) They should then understand that this is how other people feel too. Therefore we shouldn't laugh at or be cross with others when they make mistakes, but tell them not to worry – we know how it feels! We should try to help them not to make the same mistake again.

Conclude by asking the children what they have learned and how this will affect their behaviour in the future.

NOW OR LATER

■ Children could write their 'answers' to each story under appropriate headings (see right).

OBJECTIVES

To enable children to:
■ develop key skills relevant to learning and work
■ not be worried about making mistakes
■ learn from their mistakes.

CROSS-CURRICULAR LINKS

ENGLISH

Listening with understanding; formulating, clarifying and expressing ideas; writing in response to a classroom activity; drama.

Name of child in story	Mistake made	Apologizes to	Any reason for mistake?	How to put it right
Maisy	forgot sweatshirt	Mum/Dad/carer	forgetfulness	try to remember belongings

Ready to go! **IDEAS FOR PSHE**

■ Children could write their own short stories about mistakes, and how they were put right. Small groups could act out the best ones to stimulate class discussion.
■ For homework, children could ask relatives and friends for examples of their mistakes and how they rectified them.

THE WORLD OF WORK

OBJECTIVES
To enable children to:
■ start to understand the world of work
■ begin to appreciate the range of possible jobs.

CROSS-CURRICULAR LINKS

ENGLISH
Communicating effectively in speech; formulating, clarifying and expressing ideas.

RESOURCES AND CLASSROOM ORGANIZATION
You will need: one copy of photocopiable page 63 (preferably copied onto card or thick paper), cut into cards; board or flip chart; a 20-question indicator, drawn on the board (see page 63); blank cards, one for each child; a large sheet of paper; writing materials.

The whole class play a game, then end with a class discussion.

WHAT TO DO
Introduce the children to the idea of work by asking what jobs they have heard of. Sensitivity is needed here if there are children whose parents or carers are unemployed. Ask them why people go to work. (To earn money, and hopefully, because they enjoy their job.)

Explain that they are going to find out more about different jobs by playing a game as a class. Place the cards made from photocopiable page 63 on your desk, face down. Ask one child to come out, take the top card and (in whispers) to read it with you. The child then asks, 'What's my job?' and the class has to find out by asking up to 20 questions about the job. Show them the 20-question indicator on the board. Discuss what sort of questions would be appropriate and write these on the board.

Ideas might include: do you – work indoors? work in an office? make something? tell other people what to do? look after somebody or something? wear a uniform? sell something?

The child with the job card, with your help, will only be allowed to answer 'Yes' or 'No'. Each time a question is asked, a mark is shown next to the appropriate number on the 20-question indicator. The class can try to guess the job at any time, but each try counts as a question. If the class uses up all their questions/guesses, then the child with the job card 'wins'; if the class guess the job before using all 20 questions, they 'win'. Each game ends by the job description on the card being read out and discussed. More able or older children could be restricted to only ten questions.

When all the prepared cards have been used, give out the blank cards and help each child to write the name of a job they have heard of which hasn't already been used in the game. The class can then repeat the game, each child using his or her new card. Finally, ask the children to think of as many other jobs as they can. Write them down on a large sheet of paper for reference.

Ask the children what they have learned – hopefully that there are many more jobs than they realized! Ask them whether they now have some new ideas about what they might like to do in the future, and what skills they might need for them.

NOW OR LATER
■ Children could find out more about a job they would like to do, and write about it for homework.
■ Ask the children to invite relatives or friends to come in to school to talk about their job.
■ A careers adviser could come in to talk about his or her work and how they help people to prepare themselves (by getting appropriate qualifications) for the variety of possible jobs.
■ Children could collect pictures from magazines and newspapers to produce a noticeboard display collage of 'The jobs people do', and discuss the skills they might need to do them.

Name   Date

Certificate of achievement for

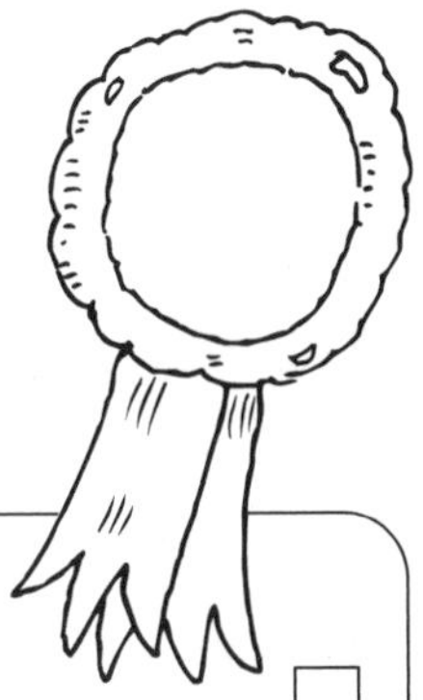

_____

My teacher and I agree that I can

Look after myself.
I can keep myself safe by _____ ☐
I can keep myself clean by _____ ☐
I can make healthy choices like _____ ☐

Work well and learn.
I can listen carefully. ☐   I can concentrate. ☐
I can ask permission to do things like _____
I can be trusted to _____
I am good at keeping the class rules. ☐   I try hard. ☐
I do my best. ☐   I don't give up easily. ☐
I can learn from my mistakes. ☐   (Everyone makes mistakes sometimes!)

Help other people.
I can help the class by _____
I can co-operate with other people. ☐   I can share. ☐
I am kind. ☐   I am polite. ☐   I like to join in. ☐
I look after other people's things. ☐   I am reliable. ☐

I have done well!
I am especially proud of _____
My teacher and I agree that I am going to try harder at
_____

Signed:
Pupil _____   Teacher _____
School and class _____

Class 3's day of mistakes!

Matthew had had a wonderful weekend. On Saturday they had visitors and they went out all day on Sunday. When he got to school on Monday he realized that he had forgotten his reading book.

Sabrina was excited because it was her birthday. The first lesson at school was maths. When she took her book to the teacher for marking, she found that she had done all her sums from the wrong page.

Sukhpal yawned. He was tired because he stayed up late the night before. He was doing his topic work. When the teacher came round to have a look, she found that Sukhpal had done his upside down!

Janine had borrowed her friend's felt-tip pens to colour in a special poster. She was busily shading in a green tree. Suddenly the tip of the pen she was using split because she was pressing too hard.

Joe had a friend home to play. They were having a great time playing games in his bedroom. Dad called up that tea was ready. The boys excitedly charged down the stairs. Joe crashed into the hall table and the leg broke. (He was OK.)

Maisy was enjoying the class visit to the local museum. It was a hot day, so she took off her sweatshirt and put it neatly in a corner. When she got back to school later, she realized that her sweatshirt was still at the museum!

■ When we make mistakes we say "Sorry" and try to put it right. For each story above, think about:

| Who should the child apologize to? | How could the child put the mistake right? | Was there a reason for the mistake? | What could the child do in the future to prevent a similar mistake? |

Ready to go! IDEAS FOR PSHE

What's my job?

You are a FARMER. You grow food crops like wheat and look after cows to produce milk.	You are a DOCTOR. You see patients and write prescriptions if necessary.
You are a SHOP ASSISTANT You sell things, put the money in the cash till and give the correct change.	You are a SECRETARY. You work in an office, use a computer and answer the telephone.
You are a LORRY DRIVER. You load goods onto your lorry, drive them to where they are needed and unload.	You are an ACTOR. You have to learn the words you will say. You can work in a theatre or on television.
You are a FACTORY WORKER. You pack tomatoes into a box as they come along a conveyor belt.	You are an AIRLINE PILOT. You talk to air traffic control and take off and land your plane safely.
You are a WARDEN of a nature reserve. You look after the wildlife, and show people around the reserve.	You are a COOK. You plan menus, and buy the ingredients to prepare and cook food for lots of people.
You are a FIRE FIGHTER. You drive a fire engine to put fires out and rescue people. You also help in other emergencies, such as a flood.	You are a CARER in a home for old people. You help people in and out of bed and chairs, serve them meals and talk to them.

1
2
3
4
5
6
7
8
9
10
11
12
13
14
15
16
17
18
19
20

NATIONAL STANDARDS FOR KEY SKILLS

The grid below will help you to identify which activities can be used to develop specific key skills, and enable you to check on the overall balance of skill development in your teaching programme. These skills are based on the QCA's *National Standards for Key Skills*.

SKILLS DEVELOPED IN SECTIONS:	1	2	3	4	5	6	7	8
				IN ACTIVITIES:				
Improving own learning and performance	2–4	1–7	1–4	1–4	1–3	1–4	1–5	1–3
Communication	1–5	1–4, 6	1–4	1–4	1–3	1, 2, 4	1–4	1–3
Problem solving	4	2, 4–6	1–4	___	3	1, 2, 4	1, 3	2
Working with others	1, 3, 4	1, 2, 4 6, 7	1, 3, 4	1–4	1–3	1–4	1, 3, 4	3
Practical skills	1, 4, 5	1–3 5, 7	1–4	2–4	1–3	1, 3	1–5	1, 3